NONPROFIT BOARD SUCCESS

HOW TO BUILD A BOARD OF DIRECTORS SO GOOD THAT EVEN THE TOP CEOS WOULD BE JEALOUS

JAMES RUELL

CONTENTS

HOW TO GET A FREE COPY OF THE ULTIMATE 4-WEEK FUNDRAISE WORKBOOK

Get free and unlimited access to the below ebook and all of my future books by joining my community.

Scan with your camera to join

INTRODUCTION

"The greatest leader is not necessarily the one who does the greatest things. He is the one that gets the people to do the greatest things."

— RONALD REAGAN

In a world where nonprofit success hinges on the efficacy of its board, you may often find yourself battling doubts. You ask, "How can I construct a board of directors so formidable that even the top CEOs would nod in approval? How do I navigate the challenges of aligning differing personalities and interests towards a common goal?" You might also ask, "What is the purpose of having a board of directors?" Or "Why do I even *need* a board of directors?"

You have so many things to worry about. Not only is your community dependent on you, but you have employees, volunteers, and vendors all counting on you too. You have a reputation to uphold, programs to evaluate, regulatory matters to resolve, and bills to pay. Amidst these complexities, one thing remains clear—building an effective, high-performing board of directors isn't just a desirable aspect of nonprofit leadership; it is a necessity—an integral pillar of your organization's success.

Your board, or soon-to-be board, holds immense potential. It serves as your nonprofit's compass, steering the organization toward its mission despite uncertainty. It's the force that shapes your strategic vision, ensures accountability, and infuses your organization with varied skill sets and perspectives. The board is your conduit for community connection and ambassadorship, magnifying your organization's voice and reach.

Moreover, a high-performing board is the bulwark of your nonprofit's sustainability, influencing everything from fundraising to reputation management. It's not just about meeting regulatory requirements or appeasing stakeholders; it's about harnessing the collective strength of dedicated individuals to power your nonprofit forward. Constructing such a board is the distinction between an organization that merely survives and one that thrives. Investing in your board is tantamount to investing in your nonprofit's legacy, impact, and ultimate success. And it's time to make that investment count.

The relationship between a nonprofit and its board can be either beneficial or detrimental. Misunderstandings about the role of board members, misalignment on finances or fundraising, or weak strategic planning capabilities can hinder your organization at every step. These challenges, however, are surmountable.

Whether you are a first-time board member unfamiliar with board governance or a nonprofit leader worried that new board members know next to nothing about being a board member–you've picked up the right book. And if your nonprofit does not have a board, this book will give you the knowledge to set one up from scratch.

Maybe you're new to governance, finding your footing on your inaugural board, and enthusiastic about contributing effectively. If you're focused on making a meaningful impact while steering clear of any missteps or conflicts, this book will guide you on performing in a board setting and working effectively with colleagues of all experience levels. It will help you identify essential skills for success and steer you clear of common mistakes.

It may be a struggle to recruit and onboard suitable board members, plan for succession, steer greener board members as they grow into their roles, or manage difficult and entrenched members. Whatever your challenges, you are not the first to face them. Don't feel alone in the struggle. Stagnation and disengagement can occur over time, but it is possible to make a breakthrough and advance. I will share simple and practical insights, so you can get what you need from your board.

You need a valuable resource on board member orientation that explains board governance and other board concepts in a simple yet logical manner, one that defines the responsibilities of board members, rules of order, bylaws, board governance, and other foundational concepts while teaching you how to effectively collaborate with other members to build a top-notch board of directors.

That is the reason I set out to write *Nonprofit Board Success*. In the following eight chapters, you will learn what a nonprofit board is, what various board roles are, good versus bad board behavior, common barriers to successful fundraising, how to monitor board performance, standout board setup secrets–and much more.

Chapters one, two, and three focus on the fundamental principles of board governance, such as the most important elements in a non-profit organization, understanding the different members of a board and their respective roles, and the core skills necessary to be an effective board member. Chapters four, five, and six detail ten nonprofits with effective boards, the role of boards in nonprofit fundraising, and how to identify and handle toxic board member behavior. Chapters seven and eight tackle setting up an audit committee and offer valuable tips for an effective nonprofit board. You'll find everything you need to know to unlock your organization's full potential through effective board governance, delivered in simple, practical language.

I'm confident the strategies I share here will serve you immensely, having had practical experience with these issues myself. I'm a charity director, finance professional, and the author of *Winning Grants: How to Write Winning Grant Proposals That Will Get You Funding for Your Nonprofit*. I have served as the director of an award-winning charity in London for several years and have led strategic decision-making driving expense and finance policy and improvements in financial sustainability. Now, I'm setting out to share this knowledge more widely with the charity sector to support nonprofits in lifting their governance game and making a bigger impact.

I have studied the best methods for creating an extraordinary nonprofit board. Helping you achieve freedom from a nonfunctional board matters deeply because I've been there myself and understand how difficult, even impossible, it seems to be able to have a board that even top CEOs will genuinely envy. Rest assured, it is possible if you follow this book's guiding principles.

This guide simplifies board orientation, making it accessible for new and seasoned members alike. It provides a clear and efficient introduction to board governance, explaining its nature, individual roles, and strategies for effective collaboration. The next time you face a difficult situation culminating in a tense board meeting, you'll know exactly what to do. We'll first explore the broader context, crucial for comprehensive understanding, before delving into practical strategies and tactics you can immediately implement. In no time, you'll grasp the duties of board membership, committee structures, methods for effective meetings, and collaboration techniques. Understanding these key elements will enable you to manage a successful nonprofit board or excel as a board member. When all these elements work seamlessly, it elevates the entire organization.

Arming you with actionable tools and skills for immediate use, this guide is about operating in the real world. Naturally, we'll delve into theoretical aspects, and there are many crucial concepts you need to grasp. But it's more important how you apply it. Ultimately, success in this area is mainly about working effectively with others and cultivating a healthy dynamic, even in challenging situations. The ability to consistently maintain best practices and overcome challenges sets successful nonprofits apart, so let's ensure you know how to respond no matter what comes up.

If you learn best by doing, as I do, I strongly suggest you get this book on Audible and listen along as you read. This dual approach will enhance your memory of the content and make it easier to recall when necessary, thus boosting your success in building an effective nonprofit board.

Are you ready to build a top-notch board of directors? Keep reading, and let's begin with the first chapter–what's the point of a board, anyway?

THE BENEFITS OF HAVING A BOARD OF DIRECTORS

"Effective leadership is not about making speeches or being liked; leadership is defined by results, not attributes."

— PETER DRUCKER

E ven a chief executive or executive director is ultimately accountable to someone. In a nonprofit, that is a board of directors. Board members are typically responsible for strategy and governance and are involved in financial decisions and key strategic relationships. This chapter will serve as an introduction to nonprofit boards to set the scene; in later chapters, we will dive into specific strategies and tactics to support you as a nonprofit board member or leader.

INTRODUCTION TO NONPROFITS

It's all in the name. A nonprofit is an organization that does not distribute profits. Nonprofits can range widely in size, from small volunteer-led nonprofits to global charities, and focus on any one of a variety of social causes in areas like health, advocacy, education, arts, etc. A nonprofit's purpose is to meet a need of a community, and that purpose is outlined in its mission statement.

Because a nonprofit is designed to benefit the public, they are afforded certain privileges, such as tax exemptions, which encourage donations and help fund their mission. Each state in the US has its own laws for incorporating non-profit organizations. Most are organized as corporations. Section 501 of the Internal Revenue Code outlines scenarios under which corporations are exempt. Nonprofits must continue to meet state or federal requirements to avoid fines and penalties and maintain their nonprofit status.

The most common types of nonprofit organizations are:

- 501(c)(3). These are essentially just charities, making up about half of all nonprofits. Organizations can qualify if they operate exclusively for religious, charitable, scientific, public safety, literary or educational purposes; to foster national or international sports competitions; or prevent cruelty to children or animals.
- 501(c)(5). These are labor unions and agricultural or horticultural associations. Their purpose is to better the conditions of those engaged in labor, agriculture, or horticulture, improve the products, and develop a higher degree of efficiency in their respective fields.
- 501(c)(6). These are business leagues and membership and trade associations. Unlike 501(c)(3) charitable organizations, they may lobby for specific interests.
- 501(c)(7), 501(c)8, and 501(c)10. These are social and recreational clubs, fraternal beneficiary societies, and domestic fraternal societies.

Once they reach a specific size, organizations must disclose certain details to the public and their regulators, such as program, administration, and fundraising expenditure reporting.

The operations of a typical nonprofit can be classified into three main categories. Firstly, the governance function is responsible for the organization's strategic direction, guidance, and controls. Effective governance relies on a productive working relationship between a board and management and is not solely restricted to board matters. Secondly, programs are how a nonprofit organization delivers on its mission, organizing and mobilizing resources–such as funds, facilities, and staff–to provide essential services. Programs are intended to benefit those served or supported. Measurable outcomes of the programs could include improved mental or physical health, preservation of land or animal life, increased literacy, etc., depending on an organization's driving purpose. Finally, central administration refers to the core staff and facilities that underpin the running of all programs. Generally, nonprofits aim to keep these costs low in proportion to program costs.

WHAT IS A NONPROFIT BOARD?

A board is the governing body of an organization; its members meet regularly to discuss and make decisions about its affairs. Generally, a board must gather with all members in attendance once a year, but most will meet more frequently throughout the year to consider and vote on organizational matters. Board members usually serve a fixed term of a few years, which may or may not be renewed, depending on a board's structure.

In the structure of a typical nonprofit, the organization is led by an executive director or chief executive. This role is accountable for the work of the nonprofit and responsible to the board of directors. The board, in turn, determines the direction and policies of the nonprofit and is held accountable to the beneficiaries and funders of the nonprofit. Unlike a nonprofit's employees who are tasked with day-to-day operations, the board provides oversight and strategy, realizing the vision and executing the mission. Board culture can vary from one nonprofit to another. Some operate almost as equals, alongside management, in a reasonably egalitarian fashion, while a more traditional approach would position the board of directors on a superior level; sometimes, staff may perceive a board as a brake or bottleneck or as rubber stampers. Board powers are laid out in the nonprofit's governing documents, for example, articles of incorporation, bylaws, and constitution.

The board comprises individuals, ideally from the community, and representatives of the nonprofit's community and beneficiaries. The board should feature a balanced mix of financial and legal competencies and strategic planning or marketing skills. Nonprofit board members are typically not compensated but are motivated by a drive to serve the community and the satisfaction derived from volunteering. Many have demanding jobs and busy family lives. In addition, a board should have one member serving as treasurer and one as secretary. We'll cover specific board roles and responsibilities in more detail later.

The board president, or chair, leads the board, facilitating meetings, providing leadership, and coordinating work. A board of directors often sets up smaller subcommittees or task forces. These are smaller subgroups of board members dedicated to carrying out specific tasks. For example, a governance committee may be appointed and charged with recruiting new board members and evaluating overall board performance. An internal affairs committee might be in charge of matters relating to personnel and finances. An external affairs committee would focus on marketing, communications, and PR–managing the nonprofit's external profile, publicizing its activities, and fundraising. Other committees can be organized to deal with projects and events as needed and disbanded afterward.

Early on, the board may consist of people who were instrumental in setting up the nonprofit or simply those with a keen interest in the mission. Nonprofits just starting may have board members who also serve in management positions, blurring the lines between governance and management. With limited staff resources, the board may necessarily be more hands-on. But typically, and ideally, board members should be independent of paid staff. The aim should be to separate those planning and setting policies from those implementing them. A nonprofit may grow or restructure its board to flex accordingly as it expands.

WHY DOES A NONPROFIT NEED A BOARD?

Every non-profit organization should have a board. They may not need to generate a profit, but they must be run efficiently, effectively, and lawfully–which a board can facilitate. A nonprofit can significantly benefit from the experience that its directors bring to the table. Board directors frequently have a wealth of experience in the nonprofit, private, or public sectors. This experience drives improvements within the nonprofit. Non-profit organizations must make the most of the resources at their disposal, and the support of a good board can maximize their reach. As board members are usually seasoned professionals who bring specialist expertise to the table, they will typically have experience and wisdom to impart that nonprofit leaders can take on, whether regarding designing programs, securing grants, gaining publicity, or whatever the case may be.

All incorporated nonprofits must have a board of directors; however, if they elect to remain unincorporated, they do not legally need to appoint a board. In the US, state regulations dictate the minimum board size required, usually between one and five members; nonprofits registered at the federal level must maintain a board of directors with at least three members. The UK's Charity Governance Code suggests a board should have between 5 and 12 trustees as good practice, but ultimately, it needs to be the right size to govern effectively.

Board members must ensure a nonprofit has a sound financial, ethical, and legal foundation. A board must know applicable laws and regulations and ensure the nonprofit meets all those requirements. For example, there may be repercussions for overpaying staff or participating in political lobbying. In the eyes of the law, a board of directors assumes the fiduciary role of the organization. It is tasked with not only opening bank accounts or filing annual reports but also approving significant financial transactions to ensure funds are being appropriately directed.

From an ethical standpoint, the board is accountable for a nonprofit's performance. Beyond meeting legal requirements, boards should be concerned with doing the right thing. Above all, a board should prioritize a nonprofit's constituents, ensuring resources are used appropriately and wisely. Individual board members have duties of care, loyalty, and obedience. Care means applying a level of concern to their board responsibilities that a prudent person would demonstrate by actively participating in meetings, contributing, and ensuring all assets and resources are used wisely. Loyalty requires board members to always place the nonprofit's interests ahead of theirs, including disclosing any conflicts of interest and not using their role for personal gain. Obedience refers to abiding by all laws and regulations at all times and ensuring the nonprofit is fulfilling its planned mission.

The board aims to ensure the nonprofit continues to meet the needs it was set up to serve. A board of directors can help a nonprofit sustain itself and grow over time by cooperating with management to set and achieve goals, articulate expectations, and measure results. Part of this is the ability to anticipate and meet community needs. A board also represents a nonprofit's stakeholders, serving as the voice of its constituency, steering the organization in a direction that serves the greater good, and keeping the mission on track. The more closely the board composition resembles the constituency, the easier this is, hence the importance of diversity of representation, which we will touch on later in this book.

Given the rapid and ongoing changes faced by today's nonprofits, it's essential for the board to focus on the broader context in which the nonprofit functions. Board members should consistently monitor industry, public sector, and political trends. They must stay informed about upcoming changes and regularly discuss them with the organization's leadership. Board members do not need to hold all the answers but should be able to ask the right questions to guide the organization forward. Even as individual staff come and go, including leadership–the board of directors remains in place. A changing of the guard does not need to impact the nonprofit's good work; a steady board with foresight ensures continuity.

TOP DUTIES OF THE BOARD

A thriving nonprofit has a clear focus and mission, backed by a solid strategy to achieve it, and the means to evaluate the effectiveness of its work. However, many nonprofits lack the time, funds, and resources for genuine strategic planning, instead spending these on addressing day-to-day issues of which there are more than enough to keep leaders busy. The board can maintain momentum by stepping back, zooming out, and bringing things back to a strategic focus rather than focusing so tightly on operational efficiencies. In addition, it can play a role in bridging the gap between strategy and execution.

Setting the direction for a nonprofit and ensuring it remains on track to advance its mission is the heart of a board's role. The board must lead on strategic planning and regularly evaluate the nonprofit's progress toward its goals. Creating realistic, actionable plans to meet the needs of those it serves is a significant and time-consuming responsibility. A comprehensive plan should encompass an overarching purpose and mission, new and existing services and programs, development and retention of donors or funding sources, staffing, and finances. As the nonprofit's operating environment changes, like when many nonprofits had to pivot their focus dramatically during the pandemic, the board should play a key role in determining the organization's response. Specifically, a board will be involved in tasks such as drafting and finalizing mission and vision statements and defining and reviewing programs or services.

A nonprofit board must also assist with securing resources to enable the execution of the plan. Board members should be involved in fundraising for the nonprofit. This could take many forms. It might include capitalizing on their connections–reaching out to their personal and professional networks to identify prospective donors, or leveraging contacts at companies that might potentially become sponsors. It could mean personally financially contributing to the nonprofit; however, donations should never be required as part of their commitment to the cause. And when the nonprofit holds fundraising events, board members should attend and encourage those they know to attend as well. Serving as a board member means acting as an advocate for the nonprofit. They should publicly and proactively take it upon themselves to spread the word about its mission, programs, and services in the community.

Board members do not need to be accounting or financial management experts, but they should know what is coming in and going out. Boards monitor the nonprofit's finances, ensure spending is appropriately managed, and that it remains in a sustainable financial position. As financial stewards, the board will review financial statements, review and approve budgets, and sign off major expenditures.

While the board will not typically get involved in recruiting, one position it must hire for as needed is the chief executive/executive director. Recall that this role serves as the conduit between the board and management and is tasked with leading the nonprofit to success. When a chief executive or executive director leaves, the board may need to step in and get more involved in day-to-day matters for a while. The board should decide what qualifications, skills, and characteristics the role calls for, then search for candidates. They must identify contenders to replace the departing individual, select the best person for the role, and determine fair compensation. Salary and benefits for this position should be attractive yet reasonable when benchmarked against other comparable nonprofits. On an ongoing basis, the board is also in charge of setting KPIs for this position and evaluating performance. They should conduct an annual performance review and assess how well the individual meets qualitative and quantitative metrics as a leader. As the chief executive/executive director reports to the board, they may bring issues to the board as needed, seeking support to handle challenging or unexpected situations and troubleshoot problems.

Succession planning is also something board members need to consider. As their positions are not permanent, members should always passively watch for potential new board members who would add value. The board of directors is also responsible for onboarding and training new members when they join, ensuring they are set up to succeed.

TYPICAL GOOD BOARD OF DIRECTOR PRACTICES

What elements drive a board towards success, effectiveness, and high functionality? The answer may appear elusive and heavily reliant on the unique characteristics of the individuals within the group. However, foundational elements such as mutual respect, trust, and transparency are indispensable, fostering an environment conducive to healthy and constructive debates. That said, there are certainly governance best practices that every board should observe, so you can avoid falling into the majority (56 percent) of nonprofits that struggle with board governance (Meehan & Jonker, 2019). Let's examine some of these now.

Leading Strategic Planning

Engaging in strategic planning is the bread and butter of the board. This includes regularly reviewing and updating the mission and vision, identifying the nonprofit's strengths and weaknesses, surveying the external landscape, and developing a plan to address any issues that may crop up *en route*. This is how the board can ensure that the organization is moving in the right direction–constantly looking around and ahead to inform its decisions and confidently steer and steward the nonprofit accordingly.

Many nonprofit boards often micromanage and focus excessively on operations, neglecting strategic considerations or delegating them to management. However, when these boards shift their focus to strategy, it dramatically enhances numerous aspects of their governance (Bambach, 2012). Strategic thinking shouldn't be reserved for annual planning or the odd "away day." Instead, every board meeting should include strategic issues for discussion. These could involve discussing news topics and external developments or inviting experts to speak on relevant topical issues. More internally oriented problems could include building a leadership pipeline and succession planning; organizational culture; recruitment and diversity; marketing; revenue and fundraising; community building and engagement; and program development and evaluation.

Example: The board should take the lead on crystallizing a clear mission and vision. Mission and vision statements bring a sense of direction that a purpose-driven organization requires at every level, from leadership to staff, volunteers, donors, and supporters. A vision statement should outline the desired future state of the nonprofit, while a mission statement should be clear, concise, and focused on goals and objectives.

Establishing and Observing Roles and Responsibilities

To ensure that the nonprofit operates efficiently, it's also essential to establish clear roles and responsibilities for each board member (more on that in Chapter 2) so that everyone knows what is expected of them and can work towards achieving the organization's goals more effectively. Part of a board's remit is strategically recruiting and retaining new members, ensuring they have diverse backgrounds, expertise, and experiences. Board members should be passionate about the organization's mission and willing to contribute their time, talents, and resources to position the nonprofit for success. The board should also prioritize retaining board members who are committed and effective–especially those who keep up to date with industry developments, demonstrate a strong understanding of how public policy affects the organizational mission, and show a knack for advocacy.

Example: Every board member should have a formal onboarding, including receiving a written position description to orient them. This enables them to understand the expectations of their role as an individual and any committees they serve on. They should engage and participate to their full ability, including attending meetings regularly–showing up prepared, reading all reports–and playing a part in succession planning for the board.

Communicating Effectively

Effective communication is a hallmark of a healthy nonprofit board. Usually, that means communicating early and often, erring on the side of overcommunication rather than under-communication, especially in times of crisis. The board is also responsible for ensuring it receives all the information it needs. The CEO should provide adequate reporting in a timely fashion, along with access to staff who can answer specialist questions as appropriate.

Example: Best practices include regularly sharing financial and operational updates with appropriate stakeholders, engaging in ethical decision-making, and holding members accountable for their actions and contributions. This fosters a culture of transparency and accountability.

Tracking Performance

Boards should regularly monitor and evaluate the nonprofit organization's performance to ensure it meets its goals and objectives. This includes assessing the success of fundraising and outreach efforts and periodically reviewing financial and operational reports. It applies to people management, specifically the chief executive or executive director, and a healthy board has solid and transparent processes around this.

BoardSource recommends the entire board approve any change to compensation, and its 2021 survey found that among the nonprofits surveyed, important factors that should drive their compensation typically include the organization's performance, their individual annual performance review, fundraising success, and external salary benchmarking. That said, it also found that only 53 percent of chief executives have had a formal written evaluation in the past year, and one in five report never having received a formal performance evaluation. In addition, the board should regularly reflect and conduct a self-assessment–evaluating its own performance and contribution.

Example: There should be a formal process for setting appropriate compensation for the chief executive or executive director role. Nearly all nonprofits (94 percent) require independent board members to evaluate the chief executive or executive director's compensation and performance. These reviews are most commonly conducted annually (BDO, 2018).

Ensuring Financial Sustainability

A board must ensure the non-profit organization is financially sustainable, meaning it has the resources to continue operating and fulfilling its mission. The board is responsible for monitoring the budget and fundraising strategies' effectiveness and ensuring that the organization is making the most of its financial resources.

Example: The entire board approves the annual budget before the start of the year and, throughout the year, monitors how actual income and expenses are tracking against that budget.

Strong Oversights In Place

The board must do its part to protect the organization, overseeing policies and processes designed to safeguard a nonprofit's resources. These could range from external to internal financial audits, to enforcing vacation policies, job rotation, expense reviews, or multiple signatures for checks. According to BDO (2018), over two-thirds of nonprofits have a whistleblower hotline and conduct annual risk assessments. Nearly a quarter have a dedicated fraud committee.

Example: A nonprofit should have written policies on conflicts of interest supported by regular disclosures, document retention and destruction, and whistle-blowing.

TYPICAL BAD BOARD OF DIRECTOR PRACTICES

Most nonprofits operate with few staff and small budgets while simultaneously facing significant, complex problems and having to find ways to resolve them. There will never be a shortage of challenges to overcome, and it is up to the board to steer the organization through. Along the way, there will be plenty of pitfalls to be avoided. Here are some common mistakes to watch out for.

Being Too Conservative

Nonprofit boards may be afraid to invest, even when the situation demands it. Nonprofits are expected to conduct their activities with high integrity and accountability and may be scrutinized for how they collect and spend funds. Corporate corruption scandals appear occasionally, and charities are not immune; nobody wants to make the headlines this way. This can lead to swinging too far in the opposite direction. However, technology and society are progressing rapidly. Updating and investing in systems, expanding programming, and even proactively bringing in outside expertise when the situation calls for it is necessary to keep up to date and ensure organizational stability. Operations and infrastructure will eventually suffer without adequate resourcing in the right areas. Playing it too safe comes with risks.

Example: Risk-averse boards may be reluctant to allocate dollars to skilled consultants even when needed, as it could be perceived as unnecessary overhead. However, chief executives are usually already wearing many hats and juggling too many things. They can't reasonably be expected to be experts in everything from finance and marketing to fundraising, HR, and program evaluation.

Getting Bogged Down In the Weeds

Another trap that is easy to fall into is focusing too much on the day-to-day details and neglecting the bigger picture. Losing sight of the overarching goals will naturally hinder progress. As previously mentioned, boards should develop a strategic plan that outlines the tactical path for staff to follow. Without a clear plan, nonprofits will struggle to achieve their goals and remain relevant. However, the importance of flexibility can't be understated; being too rigid is a common mistake. As the pace of change accelerates, a lack of strategic planning can result in a nonprofit struggling to adapt. A board that fails to remain open to new technologies, strategies, and ideas that assist an organization to grow and meet its goals will ultimately hold the nonprofit back.

Example: While the board oversees the organization, they should not micromanage staff or volunteers. Micromanaging is inherently demotivating, limits autonomy, and distracts from real issues that require attention.

Keeping Everything Behind Closed Doors

Boards that do not uphold transparency or keep open lines of communication also fail in their obligations. Internal and external communication is crucial for nonprofits, and boards that fail to communicate effectively with staff and stakeholders will hinder the organization's success. Boards that don't solicit feedback and input appropriately–looping in the wrong people at the wrong stage of a consultation process or project–or aren't transparent about finances, operations, and decision-making processes, will erode trust and credibility.

Example: Ineffective boards struggle to communicate the right things at the right time. This might look like waiting too long to share news more widely, even as rumors spring up to fill the void, or jumping the gun and making an announcement before ironing out the details to satisfy the audience.

Weak Internal Controls

According to Strategic Finance, fraud within organizations is on the rise, and nonprofits are not immune. Organizations stand to lose up to 5 percent of their annual revenue to fraud, with the median loss to nonprofits estimated at $108,000 (Snyder, Andersen & Zuber, 2017). Given their operating models and margins, nonprofits can suffer disproportionately, and the reputational impact can be particularly severe. Unfortunately, the nature of nonprofits can render them more vulnerable to fraud compared to private enterprises, especially if income streams are hard to verify and a single staffer controls day-to-day finance management. Boards frequently comprise volunteers with little financial expertise and lack the savvy to oversee strong internal controls to mitigate risk. Nonprofit boards must tread carefully to ensure their internal controls are up to the task and comply with their legal and ethical responsibilities.

Example: Without clear policies on matters such as robust reference checks, expense reviews, physical security reviews, and enforcement of vacation policies, it becomes difficult to maintain financial transparency and avoid conflicts of interest.

Paying Lip Service to Diversity

Whereas good boards have formal KPIs around diversity, equity, and inclusion (DEI); organize DEI training and discussions; engage experts to ensure equitable compensation among staff; or even publicly advocate for policies that support racial equity in the populations they serve (Nonprofit Finance Fund, 2022), many boards fall short on this front.

Diversity and inclusion should not be viewed as a tick-box exercise for a board. It isn't about meeting quotas, filling seats, or solely about gender diversity, either. It's about diversity in all forms, including race, age, and professional background. It's also about utilizing every board member's full potential, maximizing their skills and experiences. No minority board member wants to feel included solely to meet a quota, as it can undermine their contributions and diminish their sense of value and accomplishment. It would be a mistake not to value every member's perspective and invite their input.

Example: In the case of strongly hierarchical boards where senior members tend to dominate meetings, minority board members may not feel empowered or confident enough to speak up. This dynamic can be particularly challenging when trying to advance nonprofit board diversity. We'll cover best practices for meetings in the next chapter.

Lack of Connection to Communities

Finally, too many nonprofit boards are disconnected from the populations they serve. Naturally, this complicates operating in true partnership with those communities. Representation matters, and its absence naturally leads to blind spots. Boards that bear no resemblance to their target communities will ultimately struggle to understand and meet their needs without a clear understanding of the challenges they face.

Example: Almost half of the executives surveyed by BoardSource (2021) said they lacked the right board members to establish trust with the communities they serve. Only a third of boards prioritized knowledge of the community served, and just 28 percent assigned a high priority to membership within the community.

Now that you know exactly why a board is essential for non-profit organizations, the duties of board members, and how a good board differs from a bad board, you're ready to move on to learning about the roles and responsibilities of those who serve on a board of directors.

2

THE ROLES, WHY THEY'RE IMPORTANT, AND HOW TO FIND THE BEST PEOPLE

"If your actions inspire others to dream more, learn more, do more and become more, you are a leader."

— JOHN QUINCY ADAMS

Non-profit organizations play a crucial role in society, delivering essential services to vulnerable populations and addressing pressing issues such as climate change, poverty, and inequality. A nonprofit board's effectiveness is critical to the organization's success, and each member plays a unique role in achieving its goals. In this chapter, we will explore the different roles of board members and how to set up and run a successful board. We will also discuss best practices concerning recruiting and training, virtual and in-person meetings, and documents, including contracts and the code of conduct.

THE EXECUTIVE DIRECTOR AND OTHER BOARD MEMBERS

An effective executive director is at the heart of any successful nonprofit, complemented by a board of directors. While leadership is shared, critical management skills must rest with the executive director to accomplish the organization's mission. The board, in turn, must be sufficiently equipped to assess their work and assist with strategic decision making.

Executive Director: The executive director or chief executive is responsible for the organization's day-to-day operations, including implementing the nonprofit's strategic plan, managing staff and volunteers, and ensuring financial sustainability. The executive director also serves as the primary point of contact for donors, funders, and other stakeholders.

The executive director works closely with the board, regularly updating the organization's progress and finances. They serve as a liaison between the nonprofit board and its staff, relaying relevant information as needed. Every year, they should define and review the organization's challenges and opportunities alongside the board. Together, therefore, they will prioritize and set a direction.

The executive director has myriad responsibilities, including creating and implementing strategies and policies, managing the non-profit organization's budget and finances, and leading the staff and volunteers. They are accountable to the board of directors for achieving the nonprofit's goals and ensuring it operates effectively and efficiently. They also act as the face of the nonprofit and are responsible for maintaining relationships with key stakeholders.

Balancing fundraising and program management is a constant juggling act for executive directors. If too much time is spent on fundraising, programs and staff may not get the direction and coaching they need. On the other hand, if fundraising is neglected for too long, the organization's income will inevitably stagnate.

Executive directors must participate in discussions at board meetings and speak to updates on the mission and programs, staff, and finances. But an inherent conflict of interest is involved when they sit on the board–that is, serving on the governing entity that oversees their role.

A robust conflict of interest policy is essential if an executive director has a seat on the board. One approach to involve the executive director is to include them as an *ex officio*, non-voting board member; they will need to recuse themselves from votes or conversations where a conflict of interest might exist, such as certain human resources matters, budget allocations, or programming changes.

Establishing a synergistic working relationship between the executive director and the board is vital. It should be based on open communication and mutual respect to ensure the executive director has the support and resources required to lead the organization effectively, allowing the board can provide effective oversight and governance. The executive director is responsible for implementing these policies and procedures, managing resources effectively, and achieving the non-profit organization's strategic goals. In contrast, the board has a fiduciary responsibility to oversee the organization's finances, ensure compliance with legal and regulatory requirements, and establish policies and procedures that promote transparency and accountability. Both parties must work collaboratively and communicate openly to ensure that the organization is carrying out its mission and serving its stakeholders effectively. What follows is a summary of primary board roles.

Board Chair: The board chair is responsible for leading the board, setting the meeting agenda, and ensuring that the board's work is aligned with the organization's mission and goals. As the highest-ranking member, they lead board meetings, set the agenda, implement decisions, and ensure the board operates effectively. They play an essential role in developing and cultivating board culture, leading by example and modeling formal and informal norms about how the board works. As the steward of board culture, the chair's leadership will set the tone for other members and their conduct, sending a message that ripples out to management and beyond. For instance, if board meetings routinely start and finish late or if discussions degrade into personal assaults or disparaging remarks, such behavior could potentially seep into the organization's broader culture (Freeman, 2019).

The board chair also serves as the primary liaison between the board and the executive director and interacts frequently with the executive director. They may review agendas and materials, finalize press releases, and follow up on board decisions together. But a good chair will never forget that the executive director does not report directly to them (Shekshnia, 2018). Instead, the executive director reports to the collective board; as chair, they keep other board members in the loop and ensure the board provides resources and accountability to the executive director.

While the executive director is the nonprofit's public face, the chair represents and leads the board. The best chairs resist the urge to leap in with the answers and dominate the spotlight but instead remain impartial and create an environment where everyone can shine. Holding and facilitating space in this manner–knowing when to extend or wrap up a discussion, when to zoom in or out, and when to call on particular members–leads to more productive board sessions.

Other vital roles: The vice-chair supports the board chair and may lead the board if the chair is absent. The treasurer oversees the organization's assets and finances, ensuring they are sound and that financial reports are accurate and transparent. The treasurer also ensures that the nonprofit complies with financial regulations and that its practices are ethical and transparent. The secretary keeps accurate board meeting records, including minutes, reports, and other documents.

According to the Stanford Social Innovation Review, forward-thinking boards may also consider designating a chief governance officer. While this would likely be too much for the chair, it could be a responsibility assigned to the vice chair or another board member.

This role would be a catalyst for good governance, spearheading regular board self-assessment; improving new member orientation and inclusive recruiting; overseeing the board calendar; and actively monitoring external developments such as legal and social changes, including ensuring compliance with regulations (Jansen & Hatch, 2022).

Board members, in general, play their part by attending board meetings regularly, participating in committee work, and providing input and feedback on the organization's direction and activities. Each member brings unique skills, experience, and perspectives to the table, and together, they form a team that can guide the nonprofit to achieve its mission. They are crucial in fundraising, leveraging their networks and resources to raise money. Above all, board members are expected to act in the nonprofit's best interests and avoid conflicts of interest.

Board members may also serve on committees responsible for specific functions. These smaller dedicated sub-groups may oversee finance, fundraising, community outreach, governance, strategic planning, or other areas of expertise. Committee chairs are responsible for leading these committees, setting agendas, and ensuring that the committee's work is aligned with the nonprofit's goals. Committee members work closely with staff and other stakeholders, providing guidance, oversight, and leadership in their respective focus areas.

HOW TO RECRUIT BOARD MEMBERS

Overall, the board is responsible for making crucial decisions and establishing the direction of the nonprofit. While the best nonprofits recruit board members with careful consideration and hold them to high standards, 44 percent report that attracting quality leadership and board members is a high or moderate-level challenge (BDO, 2018). Let's now examine some ways to elevate your nonprofit board's approach to recruitment.

It is essential not to overload the board with too many members, which makes achieving consensus and arriving at decisions difficult. What is the ideal size for a nonprofit board? It will ultimately depend on the organization's size, complexity, mission, goals, and needs. However, as a guideline, BDO (2018) provides some insight here: nearly half of nonprofits (across all revenue levels) have more than 20 board members. Springly (2022) offers more nuanced recommendations, suggesting that most nonprofits will function optimally with eight to 14 board members and potentially fewer in the case of small organizations. Use these insights as a reference point and adjust accordingly for your circumstances. It is best to maintain at least the minimum number of board members required by law, consider which roles are necessary, and remember that greater numbers inherently mean more complexity.

When searching for new board members, there are several factors to consider. First, what expertise does the current board possess, and where are the gaps? One key best practice is to develop a comprehensive recruitment plan that outlines the organization's needs, goals, and ideal board member profile. Over half of board chairs report difficulty in finding people with the desire, time, and skills to serve on their board (BoardSource, 2021). But when organizations have a defined vision of the skills, diversity, and social networking power they desire in a board member, they attract recruits more easily. The more intentional, specific, and targeted your efforts, the more successful they are likely to be. An effective plan should include a clear timeline for recruiting new board members and will also identify the specific steps involved in the recruitment process.

A natural starting point is to leverage existing board members' relationships to identify potential candidates. Current board members can reach out to their networks to identify individuals who may be a good fit for the board. It can also be beneficial to seek recommendations from donors, volunteers, and other stakeholders who have a vested interest in the organization's success. But don't stop there. Look beyond your immediate networks and consider shoulder-tapping community leaders, outstanding program participants, and peer or partner organization leaders.

Another important consideration is the potential board member's level of engagement with the organization. Ideally, board members should be passionate about the organization's mission and committed to its success. According to nonprofits surveyed by BoardSource (2021), passion for the mission trumped all other priorities in the search for new members, followed by skill set, reputation, and knowledge of the field and communities served. Board members should also be willing to dedicate the time and resources needed to operate effectively on the board. Ideally, there should be some degree of ability and willingness to step into critical roles–looking ahead to the board's future leadership needs.

Potential board members must be vetted for the right skill sets and expertise to facilitate the achievement of a nonprofit's goals. A board lacking members with fundraising experience may want to strengthen representation in that area. If the organization is mainly focused on program development and expansion in the immediate future, recruiting members with relevant expertise in this area would be ideal.

Recruiting members to a nonprofit board can be challenging, and there are several potential pitfalls to avoid. One common mistake is recruiting board members based solely on their name recognition or social status rather than their qualifications or ability to contribute to the organization. Personal networks and financial capacity are an advantage, to be sure, but not at the expense of professional skills or community representation.

Another common pitfall is failing to consider the diversity of the board. Non-profit organizations benefit from having a diverse group of board members with different perspectives. Failure to prioritize diversity–of thought, experience, and background–can lead to groupthink and limit the board's effectiveness. The benefits of a diverse board include better decision-making, access to new and different community resources, and a new pool of potential donors (Sintetos, 2022). Establishing a diversity and inclusion committee specifically responsible for developing and implementing strategies to promote diversity and inclusion on the board is proactive. To take things even further, consider engaging a specialist recruitment agency to identify prospective hires or enforcing shorter-term limits on serving as a member, making it easier to increase board diversity (Adediran, 2022).

Once potential board members have been identified, conducting a thorough vetting process is crucial, including reviewing resumes, conducting interviews, and checking references. This process will confirm that potential board members have the right qualifications, experience, and commitment level to serve effectively on the board. To raise potential concerns, hold a candid board discussion about finalists without them present. Not every candidate will be the right fit at a given time, but retaining details of passed-over yet promising applicants for the future is worthwhile.

Finally, it is essential to provide effective onboarding for new board members. Ask existing members what would have been helpful to them when they joined the board, and explore what information would have served them during orientation, whether they felt valued, and how they could have been better supported.

Upon electing new board members, onboarding should include an orientation to the nonprofit, an overview of the board's roles and responsibilities, and a review of the organization's financials, policies, and procedures. A physical or digital welcome packet should include material on the nonprofit's background, achievements, and aspirations; current board members and staff;

reports, meeting minutes, and budget; a calendar of upcoming events; and publications on policies and procedures.

Pairing new board members with mentors to acclimate them to their roles and better understand the nonprofit's culture and history is an effective onboarding practice. New recruits will likely have questions as they get up to speed, so give them contact details for at least one key staff and board member who will offer regular check-ins, formal and informal, as they settle in. For example, checking in after each board meeting is good practice.

HOW TO RECRUIT AN EXECUTIVE DIRECTOR

Hiring and evaluating an executive director is one of the most critical decisions a nonprofit board can make. The executive director is the key leader of the organization, responsible for ensuring its mission is fulfilled and that the organization is sustainable. Similar to recruiting a new board member, when searching for an executive director, the board should create a job description that outlines the responsibilities and qualifications required for the role based on the organization's strategic plan.

Once the job description is finalized, the board should advertise the position and solicit applications. It is essential to cast your net widely and reach out to potential candidates from diverse backgrounds and experiences. The board should review applications and conduct initial interviews to narrow the pool of candidates.

A common mistake when reviewing potential applicants is to focus too heavily on technical selection criteria at the expense of other qualities such as leadership, communication, and interpersonal skills. In addition, don't fall into the trap of relying too heavily on personal connections or recommendations rather than conducting a rigorous search and evaluation process.

An executive director should have experience leading and managing organizations and a deep understanding of the nonprofit sector. They should also have excellent communication and interpersonal skills and the ability to inspire and motivate staff, volunteers, and stakeholders. In addition, the executive director should have strong financial acumen with the ability to develop and manage budgets, raise funds, and generate revenue. They should be able to build and maintain relationships with donors and other stakeholders and articulate the organization's mission and goals to various audiences.

A note on succession planning: executive directors are temporary stewards, and a board should ensure there are always contingencies for both planned and emergency transitions. That means identifying potential candidates to step up in a crisis, whether internal, external, or an existing board member. The board should also have contingency plans for the chair, with the vice chair being the second in command.

STEPS TO SETUP BOARD TRAINING

Professional development is not just for staff. Upskilling is also critical to building a strong and effective board of directors. Training can provide board members with essential knowledge, skills, and strategies to fulfill their roles successfully and contributes to building a culture of learning and continuous improvement, which can benefit the board's performance over the long term.

Non-profit organizations are subject to a variety of legal and regulatory requirements. These include fundraising regulations, tax laws, and employment laws. Training guarantees that board members know these requirements, understand their legal obligations and the ethical considerations that guide nonprofit governance, and that the organization ultimately complies with laws and regulations.

Here are the steps to follow when setting up board training:

Assess learning needs: Before setting up any training, it's essential to assess where the board needs further support. Start by reviewing the board's roles and responsibilities, evaluating its strengths and weaknesses, and identifying areas where training is required. Ask members what areas they feel they could benefit from more in-depth training. A board might collectively possess significant financial and HR expertise but have less prowess in cybersecurity. Doing this will ensure that the training is tailored to the specific needs of the nonprofit and its board members and make the best use of each individual's time.

Identify specific subjects: Based on the assessment, identify topics to be covered in the training, including governance, financial management, legal compliance, fundraising, strategic planning, and more. There may be multiple gaps and many relevant areas to cover. If so, break these up into separate training sessions. Each dedicated session should be tightly focused. Prioritize based on the most urgent needs.

Organize the training curriculum: Once the training topics have been identified, determine the best training methods for your board, such as in-person workshops, online courses, seminars, webinars, and self-study.

Consider the logistics of each, including cost, availability, and accessibility. An optimal starting point for sourcing relevant content is nonprofitready.org. If designing the training yourself, consider how best to deliver it to ensure the session is engaging, relevant, and easy to understand. Supplementary materials, such as handouts and case studies, will embed key takeaways and support the learning outcomes. Alternatively, outside experts and consultants can customize and deliver personalized training to your board.

Schedule training: Once the training materials have been developed, schedule the training sessions accordingly. Consider the availability of members and select a time that is convenient for the majority of the board. Online tools such as Doodle and StrawPoll make it easier to coordinate and vote on times and dates. It may be necessary to schedule multiple sessions to ensure all board members can attend and benefit.

THE BENEFITS OF BOARD YEARBOOKS

A board member yearbook can be a valuable tool for non-profit organizations, serving as a reference guide for current and future board members and a way to honor past board members. A yearbook also builds a sense of community among board members. It humanizes current board members by highlighting their contributions, recognizing and honoring past board members' hard work and dedication, and celebrating the organization's collective achievements.

A board member yearbook typically presents a message from the board chair or executive director and information about the organization's history, mission, and goals. It includes the names and photos of current members, along with a brief biography and their contact information. Additionally, it can be a place to recognize and thank past board members for their contributions. New board members can use the yearbook to learn more about their fellow board members, their backgrounds, and their areas of expertise.

If you create a resource like this, ensure that all board members are comfortable with having their information and photographs included in the yearbook and that any privacy concerns are addressed.

CONTRACTS AND CODE OF CONDUCT

Success in any endeavor relies on clear expectations, and using a board member contract and code of conduct will communicate them to your board members. These documents will ensure that board members understand their roles and responsibilities. A non-legally binding contract for board members effectively sets clear expectations for individual board members.

A board member contract is a written agreement between the non-profit organization and the individual on the board. The contract outlines the expectations and responsibilities of the board member and ensures that they understand and agree to fulfill these obligations. The contract typically includes information about the length of the board term, meeting attendance requirements, financial contributions, serving on committees, and conflict of interest policies. By signing a contract, board members agree to uphold all these commitments. The contract can also hold board members accountable if they fail to fulfill their duties. For a blueprint, refer to blueavocado.org for a free template.

A code of conduct is a complementary document establishing guidelines that board members agree to follow when serving on the board. The code of conduct outlines ethical standards, behavior expectations, and decision-making guidelines. The code of conduct ensures that board members act in the organization's best interests and uphold its mission and values. It is designed to promote transparency, accountability, and ethical behavior among board members and can prevent conflicts of interest, fraud, and other unethical practices. The code of conduct also builds trust with stakeholders, including donors, staff, and volunteers.

The code of conduct should be based on the nonprofit's values and ethical standards. Identify fundamental principles such as honesty, integrity, and transparency, and define expectations for board member behavior, such as avoiding conflicts of interest, treating others with respect, and maintaining confidentiality. The code of conduct should also guide decision-making, including handling conflicts of interest and ensuring that decisions are made in the organization's best interests.

MEETING ETIQUETTE AND BEST PRACTICES

Board meetings can take various formats, including in-person, teleconference, and videoconference. Generally, it is easiest if everyone is either gathered in the same physical location or dispersed. However, these days, remote and hybrid meetings are becoming more and more commonplace.

Virtual Board Meetings

Virtual meetings are more inclusive by nature. These can be held over platforms like Zoom, which has features like built-in polls, surveys, and Q&As. Ensure all members have instructions on accessing the meeting link, including the passcode or any other technical requirements. The host should initiate the meeting early and allow extra time to test all audio and video before everyone joins.

Communicate any expectations upfront around virtual conduct–should everyone have their camera on? Remain on mute unless speaking? Raise their hand to signal they wish to make a point? Message in the chat if they need to step away for a moment? Set the ground rules at the start of the meeting.

Hybrid Board Meetings

Hybrid formats are the most challenging to facilitate. However, they offer the most flexibility for all participants. When planning a hybrid meeting, consider what those merely "dialing in" need to engage properly. Remote attendees should be able to see the faces of in-person attendees, along with any physical handouts, whiteboards, etc. The aim is to design a consistent experience for all board members, regardless of platform so that everyone can access the same information.

Ensure you check in with remote board members after each topic and invite them to share their thoughts if they haven't already. It can be difficult for them to participate without disrupting the flow otherwise. Designate one in-person attendee to monitor those online and keep an eye on any connection issues that become apparent. Other in-person participants can assist if they dial in and look at their laptops when speaking, so remote attendees feel more included. This small move can do a lot to improve the dynamic.

If in-person attendance falls as hybrid meetings become the status quo, overall engagement may suffer. According to BoardPro (2021), this is common and can lead organizations to set minimum attendance requirements. If this becomes a more significant issue for your nonprofit, you must communicate that remote attendance is not a substitute for regular physical attendance.

In-Person Board Meetings

If a nonprofit is located somewhere inconvenient for board members, i.e. not close to where they live or work, consider hosting meetings at the office of a board member that is convenient for fellow trustees.

Consider accessibility. Can the space accommodate all board members comfortably, and can they all access the room easily? It is ideal if all members can be seated so that they can see each other and are not too far apart or too cramped. Refreshments also provide a welcome touch, especially if meetings are long.

General Tips

Basic meeting etiquette applies to board meetings, and it's up to the chair to enforce these, such as starting and ending on time, ensuring only one person is speaking at a time, and upholding common courtesy by limiting side conversations.

A consistent time and place: Keeping to a regular date, time, and location makes things easier for all board members. The frequency of board meetings will depend on the organization's needs and bylaws but could be held monthly, quarterly, bi-annually, or in some cases, annually. Don't assume that holding less frequent meetings is necessarily a pro. According to recruiters BoardAssist (2019), the number one criterion most board candidates specify when looking for a board to join is a board where they can truly engage and share their intellectual capital. However, in times of crisis or significant organizational changes, it may be necessary to convene for more frequent meetings. That could range from an unusual request from a prominent donor, a time-limited opportunity or proposal, or a PR crisis.

Provide pre-reading: It's common for board members to have many responsibilities and busy schedules, so allow plenty of time to read and absorb meeting materials. Aim to send out reports at least a week ahead of time so members can digest their content in advance. The executive director or chief executive should distribute these.

Prepare an agenda: Preparing beforehand is crucial to ensure that board meetings are productive and efficient. All board meetings should have a pre-established agenda that includes all items for discussion, who will present each item, and how much time is allocated. This ensures discussions stay on topic and time is not wasted. The board chair and executive director should collaborate to set the agenda and identify any reports or information required to make informed decisions.

Board meetings typically follow a set structure, including an opening statement by the board chair, approval of the previous meeting's minutes, reports from committees, a financial report, and any new or unfinished business. The agenda should distinguish items for information sharing and items requiring action or decision. Deep-dive items that warrant questions, feedback, and insights should be tackled at the start when everyone is fresh.

Keep things moving: Debate and decision-making are at the crux of a board's business, but it can be easy to get bogged down in details and sidetracked. During the meeting, the board chair should ensure that everyone can speak, that the discussion remains focused on the agenda items, and that critical points are captured in the minutes. It may be necessary to assign specific action items to individuals during the meeting and follow up with them for progress updates afterward.

Gain consensus and record decisions: The chair, as the meeting leader, is responsible for ensuring everyone has an opportunity to be heard, keeping track of who hasn't contributed, and inviting quieter board members to speak up and have their say.

Consensus-building involves reaching an agreement through discussion and collaboration among all board members. This process allows all board members to provide input, fostering a sense of ownership and commitment to the decision. Consensus-building can be time-consuming, but it is beneficial when the decision is not time-sensitive or requires input from all board members.

Some decisions require a vote and a majority or super-majority of board members to approve the decision. Board members typically use a show of hands or a roll call to vote. Quorum requirements also come into play here—the minimum number of board members required to conduct official business. Each organization's bylaws dictate the necessary quorum, which is usually a majority of the board members.

Getting the right people on your board is just the start. Beyond onboarding, investing in continued training and development is a must to avoid stagnation. We also covered best practices for in-person and virtual board meetings and how you can leverage resources like yearbooks, contracts, and codes of conduct. Next up: the seven essential skills for board members to master.

3

BOARD MEMBER SKILLS

---

*"Trust is the glue of life. It's the most essential ingre-
dient in effective communication. It's the foundational
principle that holds all relationships."*

— STEPHEN R. COVEY

Non-profit organizations rely heavily on their boards of directors to provide leadership and guidance. To do this effectively, board members must possess various essential skills to guide them to make informed decisions and lead the nonprofit toward success. Nonprofit chief executives are likelier to say they have the right people on boards regarding internal activities like strategic planning or financial and legal oversight than external leadership and ambassadorship, like fundraising and advocacy (BoardSource, 2021). In this chapter, we will explore and define the essential skills necessary for nonprofit board members to be successful in their roles. We will examine the importance of communication, problem-solving, financial management, strategic planning, and more.

TRUSTWORTHINESS

Trust is a key component for highly effective teams, including boards. Board discussions are confidential, and all members should exercise discretion accordingly. A board member should always support the board's position when speaking on the organization's behalf. They are dedicated to fulfilling the organization's mission, embodying good stewardship, demonstrating deep knowledge of those the nonprofit serves, and championing the constituents' interests.

Board members should be able to engage respectfully in discussions, remaining objective and impartial–communicating their point of view without attacking those of others. They consistently show respect for fellow board members' perspectives and value all contributions. Team members who respect each other come to trust one another and collaboratively share information. When everyone is operating from the same information, this enables informed and nuanced debate.

Disagreement does not equal disloyalty. A certain level of disagreement is normal, even healthy. Board members must be able to dissent, challenge each other, and hash things out to do their job well, inspiring and mobilizing each other towards their common goal and fostering innovation and adaptability. The ability to respectfully prod at one another's beliefs and assumptions requires a level of trust that is strong enough to weather the clash.

Sometimes, divided factions may develop within a board, and board members should tread carefully when navigating these dynamics. Board members must avoid back-channel tactics, keeping communication flowing through the executive director, who should be a strong conduit in this regard, distributing reports promptly and proactively disseminating sensitive or difficult information. However, should this happen, an anonymous survey can go a long way toward shedding light on matters or when members are uncomfortable with overstepping an executive director (Sonnenfeld, 2002).

FINANCIAL LITERACY

Not all board members come with ready-made financial nous. Even those with extensive business experience may find their know-how doesn't directly translate into the nonprofit context. But financial literacy is essential for all nonprofit board members to contribute to informed decisions about allocating resources and managing funds. The board is ultimately accountable for the organization's financial health. Board members who aren't confident in reading and interpreting financial reports should try to upskill themselves in this area.

They should understand how a profit and loss statement works and balance sheet and cash flow statement if applicable. Board members shouldn't hesitate to ask what the financial reports are telling them about the organization's financial position. For example, month-to-month or year-on-year variances may be due to timing nuances or other factors, like a programming change. Delving into the details of variances can open up necessary discussions about overall financial health.

Board members should also pay attention to indicators like revenue reliability, the track record of recurring income and regular surpluses; liquidity and liabilities; and long-term sustainability, including the capacity to steward any owned facilities (Kramer, 2018). If a board has a finance committee, those with the skills, aptitude, and interest to go deeper into the non-profit organization's financials should take the lead. If these members have a solid grasp of the assumptions built into the budget, they can run discussions around budgeting and planning.

FUNDRAISING

The contributions made by board members can be critical to the financial health of smaller nonprofits. These contributions can take several forms, such as their own personal donations or using their personal and professional networks to secure further funding. They might also dedicate their time to devising strategic plans or building a compelling narrative to support the organization's cause. Additionally, they play a crucial role in raising awareness about the organization's mission among community members. (Boardable, 2023).

If board members have a fundraising background, they may have much to share in shaping the nonprofit's fundraising activities. They would be ideal candidates to head up a development committee, especially if they have a strong reputation within the community. Board members without prior experience should still be deeply connected to the mission and able to reel off relevant talking points (the elevator pitch, in other words) in a pinch. Activities that any nonprofit board member can engage in range from writing thank you notes to donors to rating prospects, giving their endorsements to requests for funding.

Board members should be willing to tap into their networks on behalf of the nonprofit, for example, leveraging connections that could lead to corporate sponsorships. Even local businesses–smaller companies may have smaller budgets but usually more flexibility. Sometimes all it takes is a casual conversation. Support doesn't need to be strictly financial but could include in-kind donations or services. For example, a family-oriented event could lend itself to requests for help from restaurants, retailers, educational institutes, and service providers that serve parents and children.

As a board, one way to spotlight fundraising is to regularly share progress numbers or select books the board can read in tandem. This keeps successes front of mind and generates momentum.

STRATEGIC THINKING

According to the Center for Association Leadership (2019), the current dearth of strategic thinking may partly result in a positive change in the sector. The old-fashioned path to board leadership, toiling for years in committees, is falling by the wayside and opening up room for new ideas. As a result, many boards now have differing levels of experience and confidence in strategic thinking.

Modern organizations are grappling with a myriad of complex challenges. These include dealing with political and economic uncertainties, navigating regulatory updates, addressing environmental, social, and governance matters, and handling issues related to advancing technology, such as cybersecurity. Additionally, they must tackle the impact of misinformation, which can undermine trust and credibility, adapt to demographic changes, and respond to shifts in media and cultural landscapes. Nonprofit board members must keep on top of all these and think strategically to stay ahead.

Strategic thinking involves assessing nuanced situations, making future projections, forecasting trends, and making informed decisions that align with an organization's mission and long-term goals. To enhance their strategic capabilities, board members must be able to zoom out beyond day-to-day operations to consider the bigger picture when assessing opportunities and risks. They must objectively evaluate information, challenge assumptions, and consider multiple perspectives before drawing conclusions. They should be aware of cognitive biases influencing their decision-making and actively seek diverse viewpoints.

Strategic thinking involves identifying and fleshing out opportunities to create value while meeting obligations. This requires contemplating what might be around the corner, even if it isn't yet visible on the horizon. What shifts will most impact the organization and those it serves in the next few years? How can the nonprofit respond effectively, and how are other organizations responding? The most strategic board members are constantly scanning, digesting, reading, and listening to information about emerging social, political, techno-logical, legal, and economic trends and circulating summaries to share with their colleagues. They should actively stay updated with updates from the National Council of Nonprofits and seek and absorb input from other industries and fields, aware that intelligence, inspiration, and insights can come from anywhere.

According to Martinelli (2014), the critical question is: "If we could have the impact we have always desired in advancing our mission, what would this success look like in 5-10 years?" Board members must consider the institutional and community impact the nonprofit hopes to have and the type of organization it needs to become to facilitate that. Rather than sticking to how things have always been done and continuing in the same vein, board members should embrace continuously striving for improvement. Their role is to bring outside wisdom and perspective, challenging conventional thinking and stress-testing the views of management.

Modern nonprofits need to adopt a mindset of innovation and creativity. Thinking commercially or collaboratively may not come naturally to many charities. Modern boards must be willing to embrace experimentation, seize opportunities, and take well-thought-out risks. They need to gather information and brainstorm ideas, which can then be turned into actionable plans.

The ability to project scenarios 10 to 20 years into the future, forecasting changes to the organization and the environment, goes a long way. Numerous factors can impact the outcome of various situations. However, individuals with creative thinking abilities can categorize potential outcomes and identify major trends. They can consider the possible impacts and consequences of a particular line of thinking. These individuals balance immediate actions with long-term goals. They can foresee potential challenges and benefits that could either hinder progress or pose a risk to the organization's resources or reputation.

ANALYTICAL SKILLS

Analytical skills–the ability to gather, interpret, and evaluate data to make informed decisions and drive strategic initiatives–are essential for board members to master. Every individual should be able to identify patterns and trends for themselves and draw meaningful conclusions. These enable them to assess the non-profit organization's performance, the impact of programs and initiatives, and the likely outcomes of various decisions. Nonprofit board members should be adept at synthesizing qualitative and quantitative information from multiple sources, including financial reports, program evaluations, surveys, and external research. They need to be confident enough to critically evaluate the accuracy and relevance of the data to inform their recommendations. They should also encourage a culture that values data and evidence-based decision-making within the non-profit organization, encouraging staff to draw on relevant data to support their proposals and initiatives. They recognize their limitations, embrace technology solutions, or collaborate with experts to enhance the organization's analysis capabilities. Analytical skills go hand in hand with critical and strategic thinking. Analytical thinkers can break down complex problems into smaller components, examine the underlying causes, and develop practical solutions. They should also ensure that recommendations align with the non-profit organization's mission, values, and strategic goals.

DECISION MAKING

One of a board's key responsibilities is making decisions on strategic matters. To that end, members must be prepared to adopt constructive criticism and be open to revisiting assumptions. They need to be up to the task of challenging leadership and capable of holding the executive director accountable. Members will be best placed to make wise decisions once they have had the opportunity to read all reports, consider all information, hear various perspectives, and voice all questions or qualms.

Board members shouldn't be afraid to probe and always try to home in on the right questions. Open-ended questions tease out important nuances and explanations, and follow-up questions deepen everyone's understanding. Instead of accepting the status quo, board members who intentionally seek greater clarity through curiosity will lift the collective's ability to make intelligent decisions.

Exercising good judgment is a core quality for a great board member. That includes the ability to sidestep distractions and skillfully navigate delicate issues. This is usually cultivated over time, honed through experience and wise intuition. According to the Harvard Business Review, everyone benefits when management is required to justify their thinking before a decision is finalized. When members can thoroughly debate the underlying issues, the board can bring invaluable insight and analysis, resulting in better decisions than management would have made (Useem, 2006). They steer the nonprofit along the right path at a fork in the road.

Decisions must align with the non-profit organization's mission and strategy. This calls for board members to constantly re-orient to the long-term implications and impact, both for the nonprofit and those it serves, of any move so that resources are allocated effectively and the nonprofit remains focused on its core objectives. This includes ethical considerations like transparency, accountability, fairness, upholding the organization's values, and identifying and mitigating risks.

No decision can ever be made with 100 percent certainty, and board members must be comfortable operating with limited information and foresight. Leveraging structured and deliberate processes can facilitate consensus, including protocols for information gathering from various stakeholders, analysis, and discussion. These could include frameworks like SWOT analysis (Strengths, Weaknesses, Opportunities, and Threats) or cost-benefit analysis. Planning for various scenarios brings added clarity when assessing options and making choices.

If necessary, the board may need to break significant strategic decisions down into smaller chunks to address individually. The board should also follow up with management to ensure that decisions are effectively implemented and that further ripple effects are handled.

COMMUNICATION

Effective communication is the key to accomplishing tasks within a board of directors. It happens in written form through everything from short emails to formal reports, verbal and in-person discussions. Board members must be able to effectively communicate their viewpoints, articulate what they want to see happen, and explain the nuances of complex issues. This is especially important regarding issues that others may not want to hear. Members must be able to communicate clearly and concisely. That requires them to distill critical messages to their essence, avoiding jargon and using plain language that resonates with diverse audiences. They should also be mindful of their body language, tone of voice, and facial expressions, as most communication is nonverbal. All these elements should be congruent with their message and convey openness and receptiveness.

Board members should maintain an open line of communication with the executive director, which strengthens trust. Questions should always be welcomed, and individuals shouldn't hesitate to speak up with queries to clarify an issue. Asking questions gets all board members up to speed and can highlight any weaknesses in a proposal early on.

Members will do well to listen more than they speak. Listening to understand builds trust, respect, and, ultimately, consensus. This is the key to insightful, productive discussions–absorbing, engaging, and respecting the flow of the conversation. Each individual should have the chance to have their say and elaborate on their position, even in disagreement. Astute board members exercise discernment about this and wisely judge when to speak and when to sit back. They may not express an opinion on every topic, but when they do, others listen (McAllister, 2021).

Everyone must be able to leave their egos at the door and align on their shared purpose as board members. The chair, in particular, should be skilled at encouraging healthy discussion and de-escalating tension when things risk boiling over, ensuring heated debates are brought back to an appropriate temperature.

Now that you have a strong understanding of the essential skills required of nonprofit board members and a grasp of what nonprofit leaders expect, let's move on to the next chapter. We'll explore ten individual non-profit organizations and the lessons about exemplary governance to be learned from each.

4

TEN NONPROFITS TO LEARN FROM

"Imitation is not just the sincerest form of flattery - it's the sincerest form of learning."

— GEORGE BERNARD SHAW

Governance practices such as publicly listing board members on a nonprofit's website, disclosing any board compensation, documenting meetings, and auditing financials are some of the best practices a nonprofit board can implement if not already adopted. These may not be strict require-ments–charities are not required to share their meeting minutes or conflict of interest policies–but boards should aspire to have transparency. For example, Charity Navigator (2023) expects charities with over $1 million in revenue to conduct regular audits and for well-established ones to have an audit oversight committee. It also questions whether a nonprofit board has at least three members and whether more than half of those members are identified as independent, as a minimum requirement.

The following nonprofits are all examples of organizations that undertake these best practices. Guidestar identifies several key practices consistently implemented by the following ten nonprofits. These include conducting a thorough orientation for new members, necessitating all board members sign a formal agreement outlining their roles, duties, and expectations, and ensuring an inclusive recruitment process. Additionally, these successful organizations regularly evaluate the board's and chief executives' performance and periodically reassess their policies and disclosures. We will now examine the other unique ways these nonprofits exemplify governance best practices.

CYSTIC FIBROSIS FOUNDATION

The mission of the Cystic Fibrosis Foundation is to cure cystic fibrosis. It is a genetic disease affecting approximately 30,000 children and adults in the US that causes their bodies to produce thick mucus that obstructs their lungs and affects other organs. Established in 1955, the nonprofit aims to provide all sufferers the chance to lead a long and fulfilling life and does so through three workstreams.

The Cystic Fibrosis Foundation funds more innovative cystic fibrosis research than any other organization worldwide and has a network of research centers at various universities and medical schools. It has invested hundreds of millions of dollars into research and drug development, resulting in people with cystic fibrosis living longer than ever. Along with studying treatments and searching for a cure, the foundation offers specialist care for people with cystic fibrosis tailored to their needs through a nationwide network of more than 130 accredited care centers. This network combines clinical research with best-practice care; the National Institute of Health has praised it as a model of effective and efficient healthcare delivery for chronic disease. The foundation works tirelessly to ensure people with cystic fibrosis have the best resources, connecting their families with medical, educational, and financial tools and support.

So, what sets apart the board of the Cystic Fibrosis Foundation, and what can we learn from them? We can take notes from the two following points.

Electing a leader

In 2022, the Cystic Fibrosis Foundation unanimously elected KC White, who has cystic fibrosis, as its next chair. It marks the first time a person with cystic fibrosis would lead the board. As the disease was previously considered a pediatric one, this is a poignant and historic milestone. It will undoubtedly bring the board and foundation closer to its constituents and their needs.

A compelling 5-year plan

The foundation's future-focused plan spans the pillars of Cure, Care, and Community. It is clear, compelling, and can serve as a blueprint for other non-profit organizations.

- Cure: It is committed to directing the best scientific minds toward cystic fibrosis research and transformative therapies to deliver a cure and address the challenges of the advanced disease.
- Care: It is committed to enhancing the care for sufferers and producing data and evidence to support the development of the care model and network which assists clinicians and researchers who support people with cystic fibrosis over their lifespans.

- Community: It is committed to expanding and evolving its programs and services to reach more individuals and meet their needs.

Takeaway: Does your board have representation in terms of the population served? Do you have a focused and compelling vision and strategy?

CATHOLIC CHARITIES

Founded in 1910, Catholic Charities is a network that serves millions of Americans each year to reduce poverty and advocate for justice in social structures. It provides essential services to those needing counseling, senior services, health care, independent living, emergency shelter, special education, crisis support, and more.

It is ranked 13th on the Forbes list of largest US charities, meeting the average fundraising efficiency score of 91 percent (the percentage of private donations minus fundraising expenses) and charitable commitment measure of 87 percent (how much of total expenditures went directly to its charitable purpose).

Catholic Charities USA is a national membership organization, with independent Catholic Charities agencies sitting below it to provide direct services. Each

Catholic Charities agency is an individual entity for legal and operational purposes. Many have earned reaccreditation through the Council on Accreditation for Children and Family Services, certifying that programs meet best practice social service standards. We can learn the following two points from them.

Advisory boards and committees

Individual agencies' boards typically operate through several committees, keeping the board apprised of various issues. Many of these charities form partnerships with local advisory boards. These local entities are incredibly important to their communities. They lend their support and advocacy to the charity, and they're often involved in fundraising efforts. So, these advisory boards and committees strengthen the charity's governance and substantially support its mission.

Steering through change

A mission statement should always remain your North Star, along with the population you serve. According to Marlene Lao-Collins, the executive director of Catholic Charities from the Diocese of Trenton, this includes staying in your lane as much as possible: balancing the mission with client and staff needs and financial and organizational sustainability. In times of change, she says leaders must remain steady, focused, and strategic.

Establish a change management strategy to steer you through unexpected circumstances like a crisis or transitional period and how to communicate how you made your decisions. Communication with stakeholders will be paramount in such times. Anticipate how clients and services may be impacted and develop the capacity to adapt in advance. Further, management tools such as decision-making models can assist when it is necessary to pivot (Capacity Experts, 2021).

Takeaway: What subjects might your board organize dedicated committees to drive progress? How well-equipped are you to lead through change, accelerating more than ever–do you have a decision-making framework or other strategic guiding principles?

THE NATURE CONSERVANCY

The Nature Conservancy is a wide-reaching global environmental nonprofit founded from grassroots action in 1951 with over 400 scientists on staff. Its mission is to conserve the lands and waters on which all life depends, so people and nature can thrive. It boasts more than a million members and impacts conservation directly in 37 countries and a further 39 countries through partners. Its efforts to combat climate change and biodiversity loss are science-led, bringing together policy expertise, sustainable financing, and collaborative partnerships. It is ranked 15th on the Forbes list of largest US charities, with an impressive donor dependency score of minus 4 percent, meaning its annual surplus exceeded private donations. We can learn from The Nature Conservancy on the following points.

A strong guiding framework

The Nature Conservancy's work is guided by a framework known as Conservation by Design, which revolves around four elements: set goals and priorities, develop strategies, take action, and measure results. Effectiveness is measured by answering two questions: Is biodiversity improving or declining? And are our efforts having the intended impact?

The nonprofit has laid out many ambitious and well-defined goals for 2030. It is setting out to reduce or store three gigatons of CO_2 emissions yearly; provide aid to 100 million people who are at severe risk of climate emergency; conserve 4 billion hectares of ocean, 650 million hectares of land, 1 million kilometers of river systems, and 30 million hectares of lakes and wetlands; and support 45 million people whose livelihoods depend on healthy oceans, freshwater, and land.

Leveraging partnerships

Most of the nonprofit's resources are directed toward executing strategies with its partners. The Nature Conservancy works with landowners, communities, cooperatives, and businesses to establish local groups to protect land through land trusts, conservation easements, private reserves, and incentives. In the United States, easements play a significant role in strategies that avoid the necessity of outright land purchase. They involve establishing a legally binding agreement that restricts or completely prohibits development on the specified land. It allows owners to live on and use the land while protecting it for future generations. Outside the US, the organization typically works with governments, communities, and indigenous peoples to support land protection instead.

In 2021, it partnered with startup accelerator Techstars to identify and nurture new companies developing sustainable technologies. It has also run cause marketing campaigns with brands like Anthropologie, Minecraft, and Johnson & Johnson. The Nature Conservancy is also known for collaborations with sometimes seemingly unlikely partners, which it sees as vital to unlocking impact at scale. Companies it has teamed up with include Amazon, Shell, and Coca-Cola. All corporate engagements must meet its principles of corporate engagement; there must be clear conservation benefits with lasting, measurable outcomes and a direct connection to its mission.

Innovative financing and prudent management

The Nature Conservancy started with a sole Director of Investments responsible for long-term investment management. Today that has evolved to include external partnerships with outside firms and forays into investing in new asset classes and investment models, such as debt-for-nature swaps. Its Office of Investments, overseen by a Global Board Investment Committee, manages its long-term assets (its net asset base is worth nearly $8 million) via strategic execution, day-to-day monitoring, and operational due diligence. Careful management and an innovative approach to generating public and private funding continue to enable the nonprofit to deliver on its mission.

Use of data

The Nature Conservancy uses non-traditional ways of eliciting program feedback, including interviews, roundtables, and external reviews with community stakeholders. The nonprofit disaggregates the data and uses it to inform changes to its programming to meet the needs of the communities it supports.

Internally, the Nature Conservancy reviews compensation data across the organization and by staff levels to identify any racial disparities. Job satisfaction scores and retention data are also measured and examined at race, function, and team levels. It actively seeks individuals from various race backgrounds for board and executive roles. Community representation is prioritized at the board level or through a community advisory board. In 2022, the nonprofit published its first-ever diversity, equity, inclusion, and justice annual report.

Takeaway: What metrics are you measuring success by? What funding opportunities could be further explored? How do you currently seek data and feedback?

BOY SCOUTS OF AMERICA

Boy Scouts of America (BSA) was founded in 1910. It has more than 2 million youth members and nearly a million volunteers around the US. Its programs aim to prepare participants for life and are divided by age and activity: Cubs, Scouts, Venturing, and Sea Scouting. Volunteers lead each chapter, supported by local councils of volunteers and paid staff.

The board is led by a national chair, which includes four regional presidents, regularly elected members, and up to five youth members appointed by the chair. Up to 64 regular members can be elected at the annual national council meeting. The chief executive serves as board secretary and a non-voting member. The board has a variety of standing committees that align with the national council's structure.

The BSA board is required to submit an annual report to Congress and hold an annual meeting. The meeting location rotates each year. Any new appointments to the role of chair, commissioner, or chief executive take place during this meeting. So, what sets this board apart, and what can we learn? We can take notes from two points.

Use of data

BSA uses feedback to identify bright spots and gaps to enhance or remedy programs and operations and inform the development of new projects. These insights shape its understanding of community needs and areas where it is less inclusive or equitable for specific demographic groups.

Providing governance resources for local clubs

BSA offers a wealth of governance resources on its website for individual clubs. These include a board member evaluation chart, which measures factors like meeting attendance and participation, committee activity, and fundraising; a board retreat template; board orientation material; and job profile templates for executive board-level positions.

Takeaway: What opportunities are there for direct representation on the board from the community you serve? What data could inform your strategy in the future? If your organization was dispersed, what guides, resources, and templates could you provide to support various chapters and ensure consistency?

GOODWILL

Founded in Boston in 1902, Goodwill is known for its secondhand stores throughout the US and Canada; however, it also offers job training and employment placement services for individuals with disabilities, lack of education or work experience, or other disadvantages. For example, it has initiatives to support seniors and single parents. Programs are funded by its retail arm and commercial services such as packing and assembly, food preparation, and admin support. Through the Goodwill Community Foundation, it offers more than 1,000 free lessons online at learn-free.org covering technology, math, and literacy, as well as material on finding a job and career success.

Its network includes more than 150 independent Goodwill organizations, each with its own chief executive and volunteer board. The centralized Goodwill Industries International, Incorporated (GII) manages the Goodwill brand and business. It secures and distributes resources, consults on retail operations and strategic planning, offers communications and advocacy support, and competitive analysis and market research, among other services.

It is ranked 7th on the Forbes list of largest US charities, scoring above average on charitable commitment at 89 percent (how much of its total expenses went directly to its charitable purpose) and fundraising efficiency at 99 percent (the percentage of private donations minus fundraising costs). Its donor dependency score (share of donations needed to break even) is also notable, at 25 percent. What sets Goodwill apart, and what can we learn? We can take notes from two points.

Independent and localized

Each local Goodwill autonomously designs its programs based on the needs of the population it serves. More than 90 cents per dollar is spent on local job training and placement. Beneficiaries receive an individualized career and financial wellness plan; Goodwill then delivers programs and services to reach their goals, often through coordination with community and employer partners. Local leaders freely share their practices and successes with the network through online platforms, toolkits, and events.

A values-based model

The operational model of Goodwill is fundamentally based on core values, and it gauges its success by how effectively it empowers the individuals it serves. It aims to foster self-sufficient community enterprises and seeks to impact the environment positively. One of its primary corporate values is stewardship. Every local Goodwill branch contributes to its community by forming strategic partnerships and fostering innovation.

Takeaway: Regardless of where your nonprofit falls on the national to local spectrum, how closely attuned is your organization to community needs? Do your current values still resonate?

BOYS & GIRLS CLUBS

With a rich history from 1860, Boys & Girls Clubs of America is well known for its safe and affordable programs nationwide. The clubs are everywhere, from bustling cities to small towns, military bases, and Native lands. Boys & Girls Clubs offer community-based care for children and teenagers after school and in the summer. Led by 68,000 trained staff, the programs are customized for their participants' needs and interests but are intended to empower them to succeed academically and as leaders. Each year 4.6 million young people are served by Boys & Girls Clubs at more than 4,700 facilities. It is ranked 11th on the Forbes list of largest US charities, with over $5 billion in assets and a relatively low donor dependency score of 51 percent (share of donations needed to break even). These are the two points we can learn from Boys & Girls Clubs:

Use of data

Boys & Girls Clubs uses feedback to enhance or remedy programs and operations and inform the development of new projects. It surveys staff each spring and fall, seeking input on strategic direction, critical issues, and program management. As a result, it recently updated its training program, internal website, and strategic direction. The four priorities in its 2025 plan include strengthening leadership, resources, and capability; improving program quality; positioning the organization as America's premier youth development advocate; and reaching more youth so that every child can access a life-changing Boys & Girls Club experience.

Inclusivity

Boys & Girls Clubs has made a concerted effort to identify less inclusive or equitable areas across demographic groups. It has a DEI working group, including a sub-group dedicated to exploring how communications can contribute to its race equity goals, and a recent initiative in this space is to be commended.

The nonprofit worked with external consultants to pinpoint problem areas where its language or stories reinforced tropes it wanted to shift away from and to assess its approach to strength-based communication concerning similar organizations. This effort resulted in creating a strengths-based communication guide that dovetails with its broader communication strategy, including guidelines for using language related to race and ethnicity, the use of photos and imagery, and even a glossary of terms, such as *diversity*, *lived experience*, and *coded language*. The guide offers a practical framework for communicating about race and ethnicity based on expert research. Boys & Girls Clubs leaders were then trained to move from theory to practice on this complex subject as the nonprofit adopts strength-based communication nationally (Prosper Strategies, 2023).

Takeaway: How often are your organization's staff surveyed and engaged with? How could you further progress your inclusion and diversity efforts?

STEP UP FOR STUDENTS

Florida-based nonprofit Step Up For Students was founded in 2001 and has provided over a million scholarships. It gives low-income and special needs students scholarships and education savings accounts to assist with private school tuition, tutoring, therapies, or support to attend a public school outside their district.

Its oldest and biggest program is the Florida Tax Credit (FTC) Scholarship, funded through corporate tax credits; donors receive dollar-for-dollar tax credits for contributions. Step Up For Students also offers the Family Empowerment Scholarship and the Hope Scholarship. In addition, through the Family Empowerment Scholarship Unique Abilities and Reading Scholarship, the nonprofit provides education savings accounts that support a tailored learning or development plan to help students reach their full potential.

Step Up For Students is audited annually by the State Board of Education and recently received a four-star honor from Charity Navigator for the 15th year. This is the highest possible rating, and the nonprofit received a perfect score on many contributing measures, including fundraising efficiency, program expenses, transparency, and governance (Mooney, 2021). It is ranked 20th on the Forbes list of largest US charities, with a fundraising efficiency score of 100 percent and a charitable commitment measure of 99 percent, indicating minimal overheads. We can learn two points from Step Up for Students:

Use of data

This nonprofit is committed to collecting feedback from its constituents at least annually, looking for patterns based on interactions, such as service frequency or demographics. Insights are used to shape internal processes or external communication strategies to support families better. Feedback is sought in several ways, including interviews, roundtables, and reviews with community stakeholders. Community representation is prioritized at the board and advisory board levels. Diverse candidates are sought for board and executive positions. In addition, compensation data is reviewed throughout the nonprofit to pinpoint any disparities.

Innovation and accessibility

Step Up For Students is considered a leader in providing educational options to disadvantaged students. To close the achievement gap, the nonprofit recently expanded scholarship offerings to learners with special needs or who have been targets of violence or bullying. It has also invested in the scholarship application experience and the experience it provides for parents. For example, Step Up For Students has built a streamlined self-serve online portal where parents can manage scholarship or savings account funds.

Takeaway: What data could help inform your strategy in the future? Where is there room to innovate?

ST. JUDE CHILDREN'S RESEARCH HOSPITAL

As the only National Cancer Institute-designated Comprehensive Cancer Center devoted solely to children, St. Jude Children's Research Hospital's mission is finding cures and saving lives. Its remit goes beyond cancer to fighting other life-threatening diseases, like sickle cell disease and HIV/AIDS. St. Jude topped the inaugural Morning Consult list of the most trusted nonprofits of 2022 and was recently ranked an outstanding hospital for pediatric cancer care by US News & World Report (St Jude, 2022). It is ranked 3rd on the Forbes list of largest US charities, with over $9 billion in assets. We can learn three main points from St Jude Children's Research Hospital:

A tightly focused mission

St. Jude is not your typical children's hospital but a specialty institution focused on cancer and life-threatening diseases in children with highly integrated health teams. This enables doctors and scientists to do their best work and make cutting-edge discoveries faster. It is the only pediatric cancer center with a department devoted to discovering new drugs for childhood catastrophic diseases. Almost all cancer patients at St. Jude are enrolled in one or more research studies. St. Jude is a global resource and shares its breakthroughs with doctors and scientists worldwide; an example is the Pediatric Cancer Genome Project, the largest of its type. Its contributions to the field have driven the overall childhood cancer survival rate from 20 percent to more than 80 percent since its beginnings in 1962, and the hospital aims to elevate that to 90 percent.

An unwavering commitment to service

St. Jude founder, Danny Thomas, envisioned an environment where children from all backgrounds receive the treatment they need, regardless of their ability to pay. It is the only pediatric research center where families without insurance never pay for treatment, and even those with it are not asked to pay for anything not covered by insurance.

All efforts are made to ensure children maintain a routine as much as possible. An onsite school program supports their ongoing education; social workers and counselors help families, including parents and siblings. Housing, food, and transport are all free of charge.

Strategic pandemic pivots

Along with immediate adjustments to ensure staff and patient safety, St. Jude needed to adapt its fundraising efforts. According to ALSAC, the fundraising and awareness organization for the hospital, it conducts or benefits from as many as 31,000 in-person events a year. Many were canceled, while others transitioned to virtual or hybrid events to ensure continued connection with supporters. Most of its funding comes from individual philanthropic contributions, and St. Jude recognizes the importance of demonstrating impact to earn loyalty and increase generosity. St. Jude understands efficient and effective fundraising is vital to accelerating its progress.

ALSAC also shared that the pandemic did not hold back the St. Jude strategic plan. The ambitious plan triples the organization's global investment and expands work in infectious diseases, blood disorders, and neurological diseases. By adding to its pool of doctors, scientists, nurses, and support staff, St. Jude will continue to pursue growth and progress (Vanguard, 2021).

Takeaway: A defined niche can be an advantage. Are your mission and goals clearly articulated? How will you continue to serve in a post-pandemic environment?

SMITHSONIAN INSTITUTE

Founded in 1846, the Smithsonian Institution spans a group of museums and other cultural facilities that the federal government owns. It was ranked 58th on the Forbes list of best employers for diversity in 2023 and 49th on its list of largest US charities; its donor dependency ratio of minus 127 percent indicates its annual surplus of $866 million exceeded private donations of $382 million.

The Smithsonian's artistic, historical, and cultural collections hold more than 137 million artifacts and specimens. It is the world's largest museum, education, and research complex, including the iconic National Air and Space Museum, National Museum of African American History and Culture, and National Portrait Gallery. Most of the 19 institutions are found in Washington, D.C., except for two museums in New York and one in Virginia.

The administration of the Smithsonian lies with a Board of Regents. The Chief Justice and the Vice President of the US serve on the board as part of their role; the Chief Justice also serves as the Chancellor of the Smithsonian. The other members comprise three members of the Senate, three members of the House of Representatives, and nine citizens. The board terms of the elected representatives align with their terms. Two citizens must reside in the District of Columbia, and when it comes to the others, they must all hail from different states to ensure broad representation. They are appointed for a statutory term of six years and may not serve more than two successive terms. The board must meet annually but usually does four times a year in Washington, D.C. Meetings are scheduled at least a year in advance, and the April meeting is devoted to strategic matters, delving into a specific area of focus.

The board has several committees, each of which meets two to four times a year: Executive Committee; Advancement Committee; Audit and Review Committee; Compensation and Human Resources Committee; Facilities Committee; Finance Committee; Governance and Nominating Committee; Investment Committee; and Strategy, Innovation, and Technology Committee. Traditionally, each board member serves on three committees, two in the case of Congressional members, and is chair of one. Bylaws dictate how many members are required for a committee, although they can include people outside the board.

Members must be first nominated by the Governance and Nominating Committee, then elected by the board. Committee membership requires recommendation by committee chairs, endorsement by the Governance and Nominating Committee, and approval by the board before the Chancellor formally makes the appointment.

Public accountability

A public calendar of board meetings is published online, along with minutes and actions. The Smithsonian board bylaws, code of ethics, disclosure statement, and meeting procedures are also available online. After each meeting, the board chair and secretary provide an overview of key issues and decisions to the media. In addition, an annual public forum takes place each October, open to the press and the public. Board members are not compensated, although they are entitled to reimbursement for travel expenses incurred when attending meetings. However, many claim these expenses as tax deductions for charitable activities instead.

Community partnerships

The Smithsonian partners with affiliates, enabling partners to expand their educational programming using

Smithsonian content and resources. Collaborations are individually tailored and developed for each organization. In addition, the Smithsonian can sometimes offer small financial awards to affiliates for specific opportunities. This builds community capacity and means the Smithsonian can better understand how its expertise relates to those audiences and leverage this knowledge when considering its priorities.

An example of an impactful initiative of this kind includes supporting students struggling to learn from home in 2020 due to limited internet access. The Smithsonian provided educational content, puzzles, and games for a 40-page learning guide, while the USA Today Network provided printing and distribution to nonprofits around the country of 100,000 copies. A second edition followed in the winter (Sullivan, 2021).

Takeaway: Consider what criteria may be suitable as required or optional for new board members and devote one meeting each year solely to strategy. In addition, how might you engage media effectively in service of your mission? How can you leverage partnerships to extend your impact?

NEW YORK PUBLIC LIBRARY

The New York Public Library is the most extensive library system in the US and one of the biggest in the world. It serves as a free provider of education and information and has seen record levels of attendance and circulation in recent years; more than 18 million people annually in person and millions more around the globe through its online resources. It has 92 locations, including research and branch libraries, throughout the Bronx, Manhattan, and Staten Island.

Funded mainly by the city and state of New York, it operates under the direction of 44 trustees, including the Mayor, the Comptroller, and the City Council speaker. New trustees are nominated by a committee and elected by a total board vote. The board plays a crucial role in fundraising. According to President and Chief Executive Tony Marx, when selecting potential trustees, the nominating committee reviews a matrix of the board's overall makeup. It looks at the age, experience, and other attributes of existing trustees, maps those traits against the library's identified needs, and tries to find new members to fill in the expertise gaps (Travers, 2014).

Making meetings accessible

The New York Public Library maintains a public list of upcoming meetings; the calendar is posted online, including dates and times for specific committee meetings and links to join via YouTube. Committees include groups devoted to audit, capital planning and finance, compensation and talent development, development, finance, investment, nominating, and program and policy.

An unambiguous meeting policy addresses matters such as video conferencing, when in-person attendance can be excused, and accessibility to the public. For example, members participating remotely from a location not open to in-person physical attendance by the public do not count toward a quorum. For meetings that include video conferencing, public members can watch live, and recordings will be posted online within five business days. It also covers what happens during a state disaster or emergency. In addition, there is also a publicly available ethics and conflict policy.

Making knowledge accessible

Under Marx's tenure, the library has created new early literacy and after-school programs for children and teens, increased free English language classes and citizenship support, and improved services for scholars and students. Particularly during the pandemic, work to bridge the digital divide has also accelerated, increasing access to e-books and computer classes. In 2021, the library took the groundbreaking step to eliminate late fines. It also sought on-the-ground stories of underrepresented New Yorkers for a pandemic diaries project to record diverse experiences during this historic time. Another initiative included the development of tech kits for performing artists, which included an iPad equipped with a range of creative apps, a microphone, a ring light, and headphones. Library cardholders could check these out and use them to produce content remotely from their homes.

Takeaway: Even if you are not required to be directly available or accountable to the wider public, consider your board's current level of transparency. How clear are your policies around the finer details of meeting attendance? And how accessible is your organization's work to those who need it?

As you can see, some key themes have emerged in this chapter, particularly around representation, inclusion, and accessibility; use of data and insights through internal and external engagement; and clear direction concerning strategy, goals, planning, and decision-making. That now brings us to our next topic: fundraising.

5

FUNDRAISING AND THE BOARD'S ROLE

"Fundraising is the gentle art of teaching the joy of giving."

— HANK ROSSO

The responsibility of maintaining the financial viability of a non-profit organization rests with its board, with efficient fundraising playing a crucial role in this aspect. This chapter will illuminate boards' critical roles in fundraising efforts, shedding light on the common barriers that hinder successful fundraising and providing insights into running fruitful campaigns. It will give you the knowledge to create a sustainable financial future for your organization. As you'll learn, with dedication, expertise, and a clear roadmap, boards can navigate this complex fundraising terrain for the cause they serve.

ADDRESSING FUNDRAISING, THE BOARD'S NUMBER ONE CHALLENGE

According to BoardSource (2021), fundraising remains at the top of the list of board challenges. That said, it is far from the primary role of a board. The collective role is guiding and supporting strategy and monitoring progress toward fundraising goals. If the group exists, the development committee will generate an annual resource development plan. This would break down the work plan for each type of fundraising activity.

Boards are more like the driving force behind fundraising strategies. They establish the vision, set fundraising goals, and guide the organization's fundraising approach. Additionally, boards are entrusted with cultivating relationships with potential donors, leveraging their networks, and advocating for the cause, all of which are instrumental in securing the necessary resources.

According to Stanford's 2015 Survey on Board of Directors of Nonprofit Organizations, almost half of nonprofit boards require board members to fundraise; of those boards, 90 percent of respondents consider fundraising as or more important than their other obligations as directors (Jansen & Hatch, 2022). Some boards expect members to meet a specific "give or get" fundraising minimum, whether through personal giving or through donations they solicit from their contacts. A study by the Nonprofit Research Collaborative (2012) found that of boards with a giving requirement, just 35 percent have a minimum, averaging around $5,000. This typically accounted for less than 10 percent of the total funds raised. However, the proportion that communicated this at the time of board member recruitment is 91 percent. This should be laid out whenever this is the case. Every board should set clear expectations so that every member understands their responsibility in this area and is better equipped to succeed. This is best done both in writing as well as verbally. Start low if your non-profit organization is contemplating introducing a minimum board gift amount for the first time. You can always increase it over time.

Tip: Board meeting agendas should reflect priorities, which include fundraising because where attention goes, energy flows. Discussing this subject encourages members to be more invested in achieving funding goals. Allotting ten minutes to regularly talk about cultivating potential sources, brainstorming fresh strategies, or celebrating and reflecting on successes reminds everyone how essential fundraising is. Invite individuals to share their fundraising experience on other boards they've served on. When assigning fundraising tasks, make these quantifiable and concrete; for example, specify "ten personalized and signed thank you notes" and provide sample wording, note cards, etc.

FUNDRAISING PROTOCOLS

Nonprofits in the US must, before soliciting donations, check whether they need to register in a particular state. When it comes to online campaigns, donors can live anywhere. Most states currently require some form of charitable solicitation registration, some on an annual basis and some with their own requirements, although many accept the Unified Registration Statement. You may also need to submit your IRS form 990 and other materials such as audited financial statements, articles of incorporation, bylaws, etc. Some types of charitable organizations are exempt, so you will need to do due diligence.

Know the applicable requirements around providing donation receipts and follow them every time. Even for small one-off donations that may not require one and may not be claimed by donors for tax purposes, it is still good practice and good stewardship to do so. Donors expect one, and this is an opportunity to connect, engage, and show gratitude.

Consider how you interact with donors over the lifetime of that relationship. Which positive communications, such as newsletters or annual reports, are being sent to foster a connection? This is the 'development' aspect of fundraising and the core of a mutually beneficial relationship.

Tip: As a nonprofit, your organization must steer clear of electioneering or anything that might be perceived as trying to influence someone's chances at an election for public office. Know the limits of advocacy and adhere to them. While remaining nonpartisan, bringing attention and awareness to issues to improve policies and programs can be done. Avoid supporting or criticizing individuals to stay on the right side of the rules.

BARRIERS TO SUCCESSFUL FUNDRAISING

Maintaining public trust in the charitable realm remains paramount. It is an issue both for the collective field and for individual organizations. When one nonprofit makes the headlines for all the wrong reasons, that shadow is unfortunately extended to the whole industry. Non-profit organizations are meant to be trustworthy and moral.

Donors give to causes they trust, seeking assurance that their contributions will create a meaningful impact. Encourage your non-profit organization to emphasize your transparent, ethical, and responsible practices and draw a clear line to the effect of donations and their difference. Share freely, even mundane behind-the-scenes glimpses and staff profiles. Bring an element of humanity and relatability, with the bonus of keeping your organization "front of mind" as a result. Restore donors' faith and nurture their hope for a better future, spearheaded by your nonprofit.

Finding new donors is an eternal hurdle in fundraising, and it is a long-term play. Nonprofits must build visibility and awareness steadily. Guide leadership towards cultivating a consistent presence in the channels where your best prospects reside, whether online or through more personal contact, like face-to-face events. This will boost name recognition and reputation. When people are ready and willing to give, you will be on their radar or on the radar of someone they know. Word of mouth is a powerful and compounding effect, but it requires that others know your cause exists and that your ideals and values match.

Identifying new prospects, much like a private enterprise identifies its target market, is an undertaking where planning upfront pays off later. Profiling your potential donors and knowing what motivates their giving enables you to tailor clear, emotionally compelling messaging that resonates. Any successful fundraising campaign requires an engaging narrative that appeals to the heart and demonstrates the tangible difference someone can make. You can consider the many facets of the work and the multiple angles in your communications approach, but the key is narrowing it down to something easy to grasp.

Retention is the next barrier. Nurturing repeat and regular donations is not to be overlooked. Anyone can give once, but retaining them over the long haul is challenging and requires offering value in return. The exchange here is a sense of involvement. Here transparency comes to the forefront. People desire to understand how their contributions are used. The most successful non-profit organizations incorporate donors in their narratives, making them feel appreciated and integral to the cause. Regular, frequent, and personalized updates apprising them of the good their dollars are doing are always well received. Along with thank you notes, consider inviting them to become messengers and advocates on your behalf. How can you empower them to spread the word easily and encourage their networks to give?

Explicitly asking for money is not always comfortable, but a must to secure the necessary funds. Reiterate to management that it's imperative to be upfront in making solid and repeated calls to action. Avoid running campaigns that bury requests deep in the content or are coy about making the ask. Clear and direct requests are essential to move potential donors toward action.

Another common barrier? Resourcing. Most of your organization's resources are likely going toward the greater mission. If there is something you don't have time to do or learn in the fundraising process, an increasingly likely scenario as technology moves faster and faster, hire someone or find a volunteer who can pitch in. Are there possibilities to partner with like-minded organizations and leverage each other's resources, complementary skills, and strengths? Joining forces is a time-tested tactic for a reason.

You don't want to reach a standstill in your fundraising efforts, although it is inevitable at some point. Think of this as an opportunity to freshen things up and double down on re-engaging donors and regaining momentum. Always remember to celebrate the gains and progress to date as much as you focus on the work to be done.

Tip: From a risk and sustainability standpoint, remind your non-profit organization's leaders of the importance of establishing multiple income sources to smooth the fluctuations of fundraising. Corporations, foundations, governments, and even significant gifts are all avenues worth exploring.

DISSECTING BOARD RESPONSIBILITIES IN FUNDRAISING

Some may say board members have a moral responsibility to provide financial contributions, set a leading example for others, and embody their belief in the mission. Some funders are reluctant to give to organizations whose boards are not also donors. Every member of your nonprofit should thoroughly understand your organization's specific fundraising strategy. For instance, it could be that certain seasonal campaigns bring in the most returns. On the other hand, while events might boost visibility, they might not be as profitable as securing major donations. Knowing these dynamics inside out allows the board to provide valuable insights and guidance in shaping the fundraising approach each year.

Board members can also do their part by playing a role in engaging donors more closely. Hosting behind-the-scenes tours, organizing small social events, and encouraging donors to share personal stories about why they care about the cause are practical ways to deepen connections. As official hosts at events, board members play a vital role in welcoming and engaging attendees, fostering a sense of community and support, and raising the organization's profile. All this shows that aiding the fundraising arm goes beyond direct financial contributions. Board members can contribute to fundraising success by educating others about the organization's work, inviting people to volunteer or join the cause, hosting thank-you events, sharing content online, and celebrating and encouraging the fundraising team.

These actions are divided into two main categories: access (allowing the non-profit organization to reach new potential donors) and signaling (signaling the organization's value to the community by association with the cause). A board member asking personal contacts or business associates to give money, pro bono services, or in-kind resources to the cause or assessing or providing background information about prospects falls into the first category. Lending their name to communications with prospects, or reaching out to donors by phone or in writing, fall into the second bucket. Making visits personally to potential donors straddles both.

Smaller nonprofits have a higher chance of achieving their fundraising objectives when they use engagement strategies that expand their reach to potential donors. This is particularly effective when board members contribute by providing contacts, making introductions, and so on, thereby facilitating access to a broader donor base. Having a development committee at the board level is also associated with meeting fundraising goals. In contrast, larger non-profit organizations tend toward methods emphasizing personal links between board members and prospective donors. The personal touch can manifest through hosting an event at home or a business or using the board member's name in appeals or publications (Nonprofit Research Collaborative, 2012).

Unsurprisingly, the tactics that require less effort from board members (permitting to use their name, making introductions, providing contact lists) are more commonly deployed. A board member can support fundraising in many ways without actively soliciting gifts. Encourage all members to seek out a role that suits them. Inviting others to support a mission is rewarding for those who genuinely care about a mission.

Tip: Don't expect board members to instinctively know how to perform these duties, especially green ones. Provide regular and detailed guidance on how to carry out tasks, and remember that general pointers provide valuable insights, such as plug-and-play scripts and playbooks. Planning an offsite tutorial and enlisting an outside trainer can enliven the experience. Otherwise, smaller, more frequent trainings can be held throughout the year.

WORKING WITH THE FUNDRAISING STAFF

As we have established, board members can drive the fundraising vision, lead by example through their contributions, and serve as enthusiastic ambassadors to support the organization's fundraising endeavors.

Regarding grants, staff will manage the process and write the applications. Board members can contribute significantly by establishing connections within organizations that provide grants, such as foundations, government agencies, or private businesses. They can also add credibility and influence by personally attending meetings with these organizations. These personal relationships are valuable and fostered in an individual capacity. When board members engage personally, it is to the organization's benefit and reflects well on the cause.

Another easy way board members can support staff is by pitching in at the donor appreciation stage. As mentioned earlier, putting their name to outgoing communications, including thank you notes or calls, imbues them with an extra layer of authority and impact.

When distributing tasks, play to individual strengths. Individuals may be suited to acting as ambassadors, connectors, stewards, or solicitors based on their skills, connections, and temperament (Network for Good, 2023). Following this framework, a board member who is a people person, well-connected, and comfortable acting as an ambassador for the cause will be an excellent fit to be the 'face.' Someone who prefers to work more behind the scenes and has strong organizational skills may be better assigned to set up connection points and meetings with prospects and donors. Others may be ideally suited to focus on nurturing relationships with prospects and regularly expressing gratitude to loyal donors, deepening connections, and ensuring retention. Or those with the knack for sealing a deal are prime candidates for soliciting should make the ask. This is ideally suited to those who can comfortably and confidently sell the cause and navigate any questions or reservations that may arise.

And, of course, board members can voice their continued appreciation for staff efforts, celebrating their actions and results. Staff often work long hours for low pay. They will be more motivated and productive when valued and cheered on.

Fundraising is vital for nonprofits, but they frequently face barriers such as limited resources and a lack of expertise. Boards play an essential role by leveraging their circles of influence for the nonprofit's benefit, ensuring the organization has sufficient fundraising resources, and in some cases, showing direct support through personal gifts each year. Now that we have delved into this and explored common barriers and practical solutions to overcome them, you should feel empowered to navigate the fundraising landscape confidently. As we move on to the next chapter on actions, rewards, and consequences, remember that any non-profit organization can enhance its fundraising efforts and advance its mission with dedication and direction.

6

CREATING A HIGHLY PRODUCTIVE BOARD

"The strength of a nonprofit lies in the integrity of its board. How members conduct themselves determines the success of the organization."

— ANONYMOUS

The boards of non-profit organizations often consist of dedicated members who are deeply committed to achieving the organization's mission. That doesn't mean the board always agrees on how to accomplish it. It is common for tension to arise when different viewpoints are aired. A reasonable amount of disagreement can be healthy and is normal.

However, managing such situations can be difficult, especially when issues escalate to the point of causing significant disruption and distraction. So, it's time to turn our attention to actions, rewards, and consequences. Let's consider what it takes to set ground rules, identify misbehavior, maintain proper conduct among board members, and handle bad actors gracefully.

WHAT RULES TO PUT IN PLACE

Ground rules start with codifying expectations, and key documents that serve this purpose include the code of conduct and organizational bylaws. Aim to review these regularly, for instance, every other year, to ensure they are still relevant and reflect your non-profit organization's reality.

Code of Conduct

A code of conduct, also known as a statement of values or code of ethics, outlines the principles and standards for board members. This framework provides a concrete reference point for expected behavior and should connect back to the organization's mission and values. It can also serve as a guide for decision-making and related activities. It signifies a board's commitment to upholding high ethical standards and building perceived confidence and trust among employees, volunteers, and other donors.

When developing or updating your code of conduct, consider any past behavioral issues that have cropped up and address them explicitly in the policy, such as former members who may have poorly represented the organization in public settings or allowed personal views and relationships to encroach on their board responsibilities. You can also cast the net wider to fellow nonprofits. Learning from the experiences of similar organizations can also provide valuable insights when incorporating relevant language and provisions.

Essential areas to touch on include:

1. Conflicts of interest: what counts, and how will these be flagged and managed?
2. Discrimination, harassment, diversity, equity, and inclusion: what is unacceptable, expected, and ideal?
3. Whistleblowing: how should wrongdoing be reported, and how will protection be ensured?
4. Board culture: what are expectations for individual contribution, attendance, and conduct?
5. Consequences: what are repercussions or disciplinary actions that may be taken?

Bylaws

Bylaws provide the essential rules that govern the functioning of a non-profit organization. They lay out guidelines and criteria around board membership eligibility, electing members, respective roles and responsibilities (such as the duties of the chair, vice chair, treasurer, etc.), and any limit on consecutive terms someone can serve. Include the minimum and maximum number of board members, identify standing committees as applicable, and explain the rules for convening special or emergency board meetings. Bylaws also set out the frequency of meetings and the minimum for a quorum.

Be realistic in crafting these provisions, accounting for your nonprofit board's size and scope. A unanimous requirement for voting matters is unrealistic, and three-quarters may be too, but half or two-thirds may be feasible. Don't lock the board into any commitments unnecessarily. If any provisions may be a struggle to stick to, err on the side of leaving them out. For instance, instead of specifying meetings will be held on an exact date and time (e.g., the last Monday of each month), state that meetings are to follow a monthly cadence.

It's worth including certain situations requiring a board member to step down and scenarios for removal.

Usually, a two-thirds vote is needed to impeach someone for violating the code of conduct unless the whole board agrees that the individual should be removed. In this case, a vote would not need to be called.

Bylaws should contain fundamental rules and not include information subject to frequent changes; such changeable details are better suited for internal policy or procedure manuals. They must comply with applicable state laws, which may vary in requirements for items such as board selection and membership.

OVERVIEW OF RUNNING MEETINGS

Running a board meeting effectively involves following a structured process. As the first order of business, the chair must determine if a quorum is present. If not defined in the organization's charter or bylaws, then a simple majority of members suffices. The chair then begins by formally calling the meeting to order, addressing any people matters such as welcoming new or outgoing members and acknowledging guests. The board must also approve the minutes of the previous meeting. This is the time for any corrections or amendments to be addressed or any matters arising from those minutes.

From there, the meeting will move on to the rest of the agenda and systematically work through the agenda items. Some will be informational only, while other matters require actions or decisions. Reports from the executive director and any standing or special committees are presented and discussed among the board. If a committee makes a recommendation, it can be adopted by the board. There may be old business to attend to–previously discussed items ready for formal approval–as well as new business. If further discussion is needed, the chair facilitates the conversation, encouraging diverse opinions and setting time limits if required. After the discussion, the item can be voted on, amended, tabled, referred to a committee, or postponed. Members can also raise additional matters that do not require extensive discussion, such as announcements or non-urgent items, for future consideration.

To conclude the meeting, the chair closes with a thank you and officially adjourns the session. The chair should also have a follow-up discussion with the executive director to address any critical aspects before the formal record of the meeting is finalized.

EXAMPLES OF BOARD MISBEHAVIOR

Some of the most severe missteps board members commit fall under criminal offenses, sexual offenses, and financial misconduct. Actions such as theft, misuse of funds, and fraudulent practices can result in criminal charges and severe consequences. More often, misbehavior looks more like missing meetings, pursuing personal agendas, refusing to participate in fundraising efforts, mishandling confidential information, failing to fulfill assigned tasks, not disclosing conflicts of interest, overstepping boundaries by engaging in excessive lobbying and political activity, dominating or avoiding board discussions, and showing disrespectful or antagonistic behavior towards their peers or the organizational staff.

Some typical dynamics observed within board environments include domineering individuals who overpower discussions, contrarians or conspiracy theorists who seem to enjoy playing devil's advocate for the sake of it, members who prioritize personal agendas, and those with a singular issue or bone to pick. Other, more subtle signs of problematic behavior that can be harder to identify can include individuals who aren't actively contributing, are overly distracted by personal issues or perhaps burned out, resistant to new ideas or new technology, or lack sufficient knowledge to contribute to making informed decisions, while not making an effort to educate themselves.

WHAT CAUSES BOARD MISBEHAVIOR

What triggers the breakdown of board dynamics and leads to inappropriate behavior by individual members? It often comes down to one of these factors.

Lack of vision is a common culprit. Without a strong, compelling, documented strategy with buy-in across the board, the dynamics will undoubtedly falter. It is challenging to stay the course without a North Star guiding you to your destination. Similarly, attention inevitably wanders if the executive director and board chair fail to offer strong leadership and set high standards.

Most people don't inherently understand governance, and many members of nonprofit boards lack formal education or training in this area. Those uncertain about their role and responsibilities are likely to face challenges. This lack of clarity can lead to inappropriate or less-than-desirable behaviors. You'll keep hearing it repeatedly, but setting, maintaining, and upholding clear expectations is a fundamental principle that solves many problems.

Last but not least, it can be the case that a board has too little to do. A non-profit organization's board that doesn't have enough to keep it productively occupied is not a recipe for success. Agendas substantively remain the same from meeting to meeting, engendering apathy. If decisions are made mainly before meetings, and meetings are generally for rubber stamping, members will eventually feel disempowered to the point of disengaging entirely.

HOW TO DEAL WITH A TOXIC BOARD MEMBER

Addressing problematic behavior is crucial to prevent it from spreading and negatively impacting the entire board. Once dealt with, you will likely find that doing damage control has also instilled renewed vigor into a flagging board. When dealing with troublesome behavior, determine whether it stems from legitimate concerns or disruptive tendencies. Passionate engagement is acceptable if it remains respectful to others. If someone's behavior is distracting but not necessarily destructive, if their peers tolerate them without necessarily enjoying their company, and if the board still gets things done effectively overall, then this may not fall into the category of conduct that requires immediate addressing. On the other hand, if the board's ability to do its job is affected, tension runs high at meetings, and too much time is spent mediating between individuals, this points to a destructive dynamic that is not in the board's or the organization's best interests.

A troublemaker sowing dissent in one person's eyes may be a lively participant in another person's view. A board member may be seeking more information directly from staff to build a clearer picture of an issue for themselves, or they may be out to recruit allies and undermine the executive director. Anonymous surveys gauge whether factions are forming, while board self-assessments and peer reviews can provide valuable perspectives on individual and collective performance.

Once you have determined further action is needed, a meeting should be arranged between the individual and the board chair. Name the observed behaviors on their part and the impact on their fellow directors, and suggest a more practical approach they could try instead. It is essential to approach these situations professionally, treating them just as you would address an employee's poor performance. Keep the focus on the betterment of the organization. During these interventions, communicate how the behavior falls short of board member requirements, referring to the code of conduct. Emphasize the negative impact on decision-making and the nonprofit's future, and discuss the plan of action if matters do not change, including the possibility of removal.

If an intervention fails to yield improvement, the next step is a group intervention involving the entire board.

The group can air their concerns and suggest alternatives, but this expectation requires firm moderation to ensure all perspectives are heard orderly. For instance, you may give individuals time to speak and state their case before ceding to the next person.

If things still don't improve, and the board member's term is nearing its end, one course of action is to request their resignation before the next election. Alternatively, turn to the bylaws to determine voting requirements to remove the member. If removal is not feasible according to the bylaws, limit the individual's involvement in board matters while remembering they are still a voting member. Removing a board member from their position should be a last resort. A direct request to step down can be uncomfortable, but if matters have deteriorated to this point, it is necessary and shouldn't come as a surprise.

Consider including provisions in the bylaws as potential mechanisms for dealing with unproductive or disruptive members. Repeat offenders demonstrating particularly egregious behavior could be dealt with through impeachment. Term limits also bake in a natural endpoint for all members. That said, term limits should not be relied upon for this purpose. Toxic board members should be confronted and dealt with proactively rather than sitting back and waiting for their time to be up.

HOW TO DEAL WITH AN UNPRODUCTIVE BOARD MEMBER

Taking action and remaining optimistic about finding a resolution is essential when dealing with an unproductive board member. Nonparticipating members can have a demoralizing effect on even the most effective boards, and things are likely only to get worse, not better, if left unchecked.

Start by reviewing whether expectations were communicated to the board member when they joined. The first port of call should be a friendly conversation, refreshing them on the obligations expected of all board members. You can explain how other board members go about fulfilling their responsibilities. Keep the conversation formal and respectful, and avoid holding it before or after a board meeting. Approach the meeting with curiosity, care, an open mind, and a problem-solving mentality.

Tactfully explore whether they have the time and capacity to be an active participant right now, expressing concern about how things have been going recently and questioning whether temporary factors are at play. Personal circumstances, such as health or family issues, may be impacting an individual board member's level of participation. If that is the case, it can be appropriate to reduce their workload by redistributing responsibilities to other board members. For example, having someone else generate a first draft of a project they were working on based on their existing notes.

Get clear on any specific actions they will take from here. This calls for a blend of empathy and firmness concerning mutual expectations. The board member must understand their responsibilities and determine if they can fulfill them. If they need a temporary leave of absence due to health, work, or other reasons, accommodate their needs and allow them to return when ready. If they decide to step back, express gratitude on behalf of the board for their contributions. Their resignation should enable them to leave with dignity, leaving all parties with positive feelings.

SYSTEMIC PROBLEMS THAT CAUSE LOW PARTICIPATION

Sometimes, the problem of board nonparticipation is rooted in systemic issues. This calls for more investigation. A well-designed survey identifies the factors behind low participation. Dig into what changes would make attending easier, such as frequency, day or time, or length of board meetings. There may be other barriers or even off-putting factors, or there may simply be a lack of compelling reasons to attend. Sometimes addressing lackluster participation requires direct, probing conversations to determine the root causes. Informal chats over lunch or coffee with individuals can shed light on matters. Consider discussing the possible reasons behind superficial board participation and explore strategies to engage members more deeply.

Once the chair has gathered and synthesized insights into the underlying issues, the board may need to adjust expectations by reducing individual responsibilities and restructuring tasks or committees to suit the capacity of busy board members.

A "climate" assessment marks an ideal time to review the requirements and expectations of all board members through a broader board discussion where core expectations are reassessed and reaffirmed. Together, check the minimum expectations for all board members, and encourage individuals to suggest ways to contribute beyond those requirements. Gentle reminders about the unified vision of the overall board may get the board back on track and prevent future derailments.

HOW TO IMPROVE ATTENDANCE

Many boards eventually face the challenge of meeting attendance. At the very least, a minimum number is required for a quorum, and beyond that, a flourishing board requires engaged participants who will show up and do more than fill a seat. That is why every nonprofit organization should have a board meeting attendance clause as part of its bylaws, which outlines any repercussions for noncompliance. For instance, missing more than a certain number of meetings in a year may cause removal from the board.

Tackling this head-on begins with understanding the reason for poor attendance. Most board members fail to attend meetings because they perceive them as repetitive, inefficient, predictable, tedious, or overly operational. Give everyone a chance to have their say through an anonymous survey. Find out what they perceive as worthwhile and a waste of time.

Some general tips to kickstart fresh interest in meetings are basic but often overlooked. Start and end on time. Early arrival can be incentivized by serving refreshments beforehand. The agenda should assign a certain amount of time to each line item, which should be adhered to, and begin with the most important subjects first.

Board meetings often become a rut of dry reporting and business as usual. To revive them, consider recasting the agenda to echo the pillars of the non-profit organization's strategic plan. That means reports from the executive director, staff, and committees should also clearly relate to the strategy, and as a result, so will the talking points. Additionally, try including a standard line item as the last agenda point devoted to changes in the strategic environment. This opens up discussions on key trends to be aware of that may have implications for the organization.

If many committees are vying for time, you may take it further and reduce committee reports to one-page summaries. This frees up time for discussions and decisions on major issues. The chair must facilitate and moderate to allow everyone to be heard. The more time spent listening to members other than the chair or executive director, and the more decisions made in meetings, the better. These are indications that the board is functioning efficiently.

Hearing various fresh voices will improve engagement and keep board members interested. For example, once a quarter, a staff member could present at a meeting about the strategic issues they are dealing with in their area of activity. Bring in external guest speakers from other nonprofits, funding organizations, government agencies, etc.

Implementing some or all of these techniques will spark refreshed interest from board members who have become disengaged. Reducing monotony and making meetings more meaningful is the key. Instead of forcing compliance through attendance, you establish a 'pull' factor that motivates and compels members to attend to avoid missing out on significant and stimulating debate.

No board is without flaws; any group of humans working together sometimes experiences discord. Interpersonal conflict is bound to arise at some point. Whether dealing with unproductive or toxic individuals or more ingrained systemic stagnation, you can determine what's going on, correct course, and improve the board's culture with curiosity, patience, and diligence. You've gained some pointers in this chapter about nurturing a passionate yet productive nonprofit board; next, we will discuss setting up key committees for your board.

7

WHY AUDIT AND COMPENSATION COMMITTEES ARE ESSENTIAL

"The duty of a good steward is to manage resources with transparency and full accountability."

— J. OSWALD SANDERS

K ey non-profit organization board responsibilities include managing risks, regulatory compliance, and financial health. Audit and compensation committees can achieve these goals. Regardless of size or revenue, most nonprofits questioned in a BDO survey had audit and finance board committees. As for compensation committees, these were common among most larger nonprofits but less so in small or mid-size organizations (BDO, 2018). We'll speak briefly to compensation committees here but concentrate mainly on the audit function.

WHAT IS A COMPENSATION COMMITTEE?

A compensation committee is responsible for reviewing all forms of compensation, including salary and other benefits like insurance, allowances, or use of company assets, in a non-profit organization. This especially applies to executive staff, who may qualify for certain benefits unavailable to lower-ranking employees.

Committee members should have a grasp of compensation, employee benefits, and the need for considered analysis in this area. Human resources staff within the non-profit organization may advise the committee but should not serve on it. There may be times when the compensation committee has reason to collaborate with the audit committee; therefore, the chair of the former should not serve on the latter.

The committee might be responsible for all employee compensation in a smaller nonprofit. In most cases, however, a compensation committee approves ranges for only senior staff, and the executive director sets compensation for the rest of the staff. This supports the delineation between board oversight and management matters. The committee will report back to the board on its work, especially whenever any compensation decisions or changes are made (Johnson, 2006).

Much like an audit committee, a compensation committee works best with independence. This committee considers equity, measurement systems, an overarching approach, and repeatable processes concerning compensation. As an advisory committee, this group may seek outside input and ask for an audit of its work occasionally (Wire, 2022). Members should have some degree of experience or knowledge in this area, as it is up to this committee to ask questions about how leadership performance is assessed and how it can be teased out from broader organizational objectives. That said, they also need to consider the nonprofit's values and uphold those in the context of compensation.

WHAT IS AN AUDIT COMMITTEE?

Audit committees are tasked with providing oversight for the non-profit organization's independent audit. This is one of the major operating committees of a board, given its role concerning financial reporting and disclosure. An audit committee, rather than a standing committee, may alternatively be a task force that assembles and dissolves as needed, meeting only when required. The committee does not get involved in day-to-day accounting operations. It governs the independent audit process, typically hiring and assessing the independent auditor, and will report to the committee, not management. The committee is usually accountable for following up and implementing auditor recommendations.

The audit committee is the body that reviews the non-profit organization's financial reporting, disclosures, compliance, internal control, and risk processes, identifying any weaknesses and addressing them. In working closely with independent auditors, the committee can ensure the non-profit organization's books are accurate and that no conflicts of interest are at play.

After appointing an independent auditor, the committee will work closely with staff to prepare sufficiently for the independent audit. The audit committee will frequently communicate with the organization's chief financial officer or equivalent. If there is an internal audit function, the committee will work with that department similarly to how it works with external auditors. The committee is supported by this function, receiving much information from it. The committee will review and approve the internal audit work plan. The internal department should be accountable to the committee, and the committee should evaluate its performance, making sure it meets the organization's needs.

The audit committee is responsible for asking management and independent auditors questions throughout the process to get the information needed to evaluate matters properly. Members should familiarize themselves with previous years' reporting and its recommendations. The audit committee will commonly meet two to four times each year. At the very least, one planning meeting should be held with the external auditor and one review meeting. It is best practice for internal audit to attend all committee meetings, including any with external auditors (Grant Thornton, 2016).

The audit committee receives reports directly from the independent auditors. It will review the findings internally, as well as with management. Finally, the audit committee should present the external audit findings to the board, ensuring any recommendations within the report are fully understood before formally accepting them. The committee may also make recommendations for adjusting reporting or management practices for the future. The following year, the audit committee may need to work with management on any areas noted by the audit as needing attention to ensure follow-up actions are adequate and produce the intended results.

THE IMPORTANCE OF AN AUDIT COMMITTEE

An audit committee plays a central role in reporting and risk management, upholding credibility and confidence. Transparency and integrity are ensured through its efforts. This group is primarily concerned with three key elements of independence. First, an external auditor's opinion must not be influenced by management. An internal auditor must also be equally independent and able to report freely to the committee. Finally, management and the board must be independent of vendors. In providing oversight of these controls, the audit committee promotes ethical and effective stewardship and trust in a non-profit organization.

Risk is also the work of audit committees, from ensuring the safeguarding of assets to planning for and managing various organizational risks. This can range from auditing adherence to donor and grantor requirement or conflict of interest policies. Naturally, ensuring compliance with any regulatory standards also falls under the purview of the audit committee. But often, other matters fall to the audit committee to oversee, like disaster planning or vulnerability to technology, because there isn't a discrete committee to handle it.

The committee may also act as a *de facto* ombudsperson for the non-profit organization, charged with reviewing or addressing any complaints about financial mismanagement from whistleblowers. As you can see, its remit extends into many areas. Therefore, it's essential to have a charter that lays out the committee's scope of responsibility and authority to benefit the entire board.

CHOOSING AUDIT COMMITTEE MEMBERS

Despite their skills and experience, a board treasurer should not serve on the audit committee to reduce potential conflicts of interest. Independence also requires that no member is employed by the non-profit organization directly or the audit firm. Employees of either would not be placed to make neutral observations and judgments about accounts, procedures, and performance.

However, at least one audit committee member should have a solid financial background. The committee should typically consist of three to five members but will have at least two or three. Those members should be able to demonstrate a solid level of financial literacy and be familiar with standard financial terms and accounting concepts. The Council of Nonprofits (2023) states that at least one committee member should be intimately familiar with the nonprofit auditing process. The committee, if not the whole board, should be comfortable with basic accounting standards applicable to charitable organizations, developing and implementing internal financial controls and procedures, and evaluating basic financial statements. That includes the ability to interpret a balance sheet, profit and loss statement, and cash flow statement.

With the non-profit organization itself, the audit committee members must understand its operations and will need to understand relevant operational and financial risks and compliance issues. Other diverse perspectives are also valuable regarding the fringes of the committee's mandate, such as assessing IT, sustainability, or conduct risk.

Characteristics to look for in all audit committee members include an inquisitive mind and a sense of healthy skepticism, as the role of this group is often to challenge findings and assumptions. Members should be meticulous in their attention to detail. And because the commitment required of audit committee members can be significant, members must be able to dedicate the necessary time.

Some states allow standing committees to include non-board members, while others require committees to consist only of board members. Ensure that appointments to your audit committee are structured to be consistent with any relevant law.

BOARD COMMUNICATIONS

The free flow of information and effective communication are central to the success of an audit committee. This encompasses written and verbal, as well as formal and informal communications, including with internal and external audit and the wider board. The audit committee will be liaising regularly with stakeholders between committee meetings.

The audit committee needs continuous access to teams within the organization and the auditors, while remaining within its governance remit. It requires concise, timely material from management and finance to do its job. The volume of information presented for review adds up fast, and a committee providing oversight needs succinct communications that cut through and highlight the essentials.

Best practices for an audit committee include hosting a prep meeting or call between the committee chair and the auditor before each committee meeting and creating summaries to circulate beforehand (Tugman & Leka, 2019). Meetings should be conducted at an appropriate frequency and follow an agenda, with sufficient time to discuss each item on the schedule. The committee should also seek input from the management team about any newly identified risks. They should be forward-looking, considering potential challenges and opportunities within the organization's framework and the wider environment.

The audit committee is responsible for communicating with the board about its activities. Rather than the board giving the committee's reports a seal of approval, there should be robust deliberation on its work and any topics that warrant the wider board's attention. Additionally, suppose the committee would benefit from more education to better understand the audit function and reporting. In that case, this represents an excellent opportunity to invite the auditors to present at a board meeting so directors can hear straight from them.

USING AN EXTERNAL AUDITOR

An external audit of financial statements is conducted to see whether they represent an accurate and fair view of the company's position, operations, and cash flow, in line with generally accepted accounting principles. The auditor must closely examine the relevant documents and communicate its accounting policies and practices, estimates, and any significant or unusual transactions to the non-profit organization. The external auditor should provide a draft report early on and proactively discuss contentious or complex matters.

According to BDO (2018), non-profit organizations have engaged their current audit firms for an average of 8.5 years, with 15 percent having retained the same audit firm for 15 years or more. Less than a third have a policy on mandatory audit firm partner rotation. But a typical procedure, held by just over half of survey respondents, is to have a competitive bid process after five years or more.

When engaging an external auditor, these are the main areas to cover, from their credentials to their view of the wider operating landscape. What are their qualifications to perform the work and their service approach? What risks do they see concerning the financial statements and controls, and what is their audit plan? What are their disclosures and observations in terms of the overall reporting quality? What matters of note must they bring to the audit committee's attention?

MONITORING COMMITTEE PERFORMANCE

An audit committee is accountable for monitoring the external auditor's performance–their level of responsiveness, staffing, specific industry expertise, ability to address issues unique to the non-profit organization, and overall value add. Based on the committee's evaluation, they may recommend retaining the same auditor next year or using a different firm. As part of this reflection process, the audit committee must audit itself and consider how efficient the process was, how much disruption the non-profit organization faced, and how thorough the committee's report was. The audit committee should evaluate how it handled coordinating matters between itself, the external auditor, and the internal auditor, aiming to eliminate duplication, reduce cost, and optimize efficiency.

How effectively the audit committee interacts with the board should also be evaluated. We have already touched on board communications; the committee should generate digestible summaries to guide discussions and be equipped to lead in-depth conversations, with the flexibility to add extras as they arise. Deloitte (2023) produced a comprehensive charity audit committee performance checklist, which includes key points such as maintaining direct reporting lines between the internal audit and the committee; regular and yearly reporting back to the board; regularly reviewing the risk register and action plan; and having a process to stay abreast of relevant legal and regulatory issues.

Finally, the audit committee should conduct succession planning as part of its job. Who is in line to chair the committee in the coming years? Are the right members currently serving on it? While the audit committee relies on external expertise, ongoing professional education may be necessary to ensure members keep up with emerging issues, latest developments, new technologies, and best practices.

This chapter offered a thorough guide to standing up an audit committee, explaining its importance and giving guidance about setting one up for success and monitoring its performance. Now, let's move on to the final chapter in this book, which weaves together various threads and ties up loose ends.

8

BONUS TIPS AND EXTRA CONSIDERATIONS

"Leadership is not about being in charge. It's about taking care of those in your charge."

— SIMON SINEK

So far, we've covered a lot. From establishing the role of a board and its members to learning from long-running, successful nonprofits, all the way through navigating fundraising, committees, and maintaining a functional board of directors, you are now well equipped to go forth and lead. But before you do, I want to give you a few final lessons. This chapter contains some extra tips and advice to remember going forward.

RISKS OF THE PAST CEO'S LINGERING PRESENCE

The ghost of a former CEO or executive director can linger after their departure. In some cases, they physically remain, staying on in some capacity. If they were the organization's founder, this adds an extra layer of complexity. As the Stanford Social Innovation Review reports, nonprofit boards more commonly design a continuing role for founders (45 percent) than arrange a clean break (31 percent). Unlike something program-related, the former founder is best suited to fundraising and organizational strategy in a board capacity. In cases where founders stayed, most reported that founders made positive contributions–such as ambassadorial visits, advocacy, fundraising, and mentoring the successor–and three-quarters thought the benefits were worthwhile. Conversely, almost half of the other organizations stated things would have gone better had the founder played a continuing role (Tuomala, Yeh & Smith, 2018).

This can work if the founder is prepared to play a different role, genuinely wants their successor to thrive, and maintains engagement. But the board must lay the groundwork to define an appropriate role for the outgoing founder and oversee that transitional process.

Regardless of whether the outgoing head is a founder or not, some principles apply. The board should evaluate how well the outgoing and incoming leaders work together. If the new candidate is internal, that relationship is more established and easier to gauge. This is why succession planning is a long game and should be an evergreen concern. At the very least, this should be a topic of discussion at annual reviews, strategic planning, and tenure milestones.

Ensure the replacement has time to settle in and establish their leadership, especially if there will be any shifts in strategy or staffing. The outgoing CEO should keep a low profile during this initial period. The two must understand how decisions will be made this time. The board should have a process for managing any conflict that arises between the two, as well as any delicate external relationships. For example, if funders are particularly close to the former CEO, encourage them to introduce those critical outside parties to their successor to begin transitioning over the relationship. The board must anticipate the cultural and political elements of the transition and monitor these, along with the operational aspects.

Quigley & Hambrick (2012) suggest that the consequence of former CEOs remaining on boards is that their successors are restricted in their discretion when making appropriate strategic changes. To maximize the odds of success and smooth the transition, boards must strike the right balance of involvement. Board members will not be present daily and may want to give the new leader a respectable amount of space, but they risk being too distant. The majority of new chief executives, whether promoted internally or hired from outside, perceive their boards as less involved than they should be (Ciampa, 2016). Board members can maintain an optimal energy level by proactively offering clear guidance on expectations from their end. What frequency and detail of communication is expected? And conversely, what does the new leader need or want, and what would enable a productive working relationship in their view?

SHOULD THE BOARD MEDDLE IN DAY-TO-DAY AFFAIRS?

Nonprofit directors are often volunteers passionate about the cause, which can lead to them overstepping. When they forget boundaries and begin getting into the organization's day-to-day activities, this, unfortunately, causes friction with staff while simultaneously stealing time and energy from governance. Instead of rubber-stamping and cheerleading boards, micromanaging boards stray too far from governance and into management, disempowering staff in their intrusion.

The board has the right to know about anything happening within an organization and should take an appropriate interest in operations. But when they get involved in the execution of the strategy, that is a sign they have crossed the line. Board members should not be directing staff or making decisions on their behalf. They may do this in their day jobs, but in this capacity, their function is to observe and advise. Their power and influence stems from the board as a collective whole.

To guard and protect staff autonomy while keeping board members apprised, define relationships and responsibilities in charters, standards, or codes of conduct. Ensure the strategic plan is used as a lens to guide board decisions, actions, and staff. When boundaries are unclear, it's hard to differentiate between policy, strategy, and implementation or assess if the issue will have a long-term effect.

DISCOURAGING DIVISIONS AND SMEAR CAMPAIGNS

Distrust can breed division among boards. For example, if an executive director fails to provide enough information on time, board members may seek it out through back channels. Or they may tap individual staff simply because they are pursuing their own agendas. Some directors may be concerned only about one aspect of the nonprofit and not interested in how all the areas fit together holistically. Of course, those with particular expertise or interest in one place should support and advocate accordingly, but not at the expense of all others. It is not a competition for resources among pet projects. Otherwise, a board risks breaking down into warring camps.

Other complicated dynamics may emerge due to personal relationships or influence, such as board members' loyalty to a chair or executive director. A domineering chair or executive director may manipulate discussions in service of their agenda. Such divisive styles and personalities can contribute to cliques forming—something to avoid.

To build a healthy climate of trust and respect, the CEO should share difficult updates promptly and candidly, giving access to staff who can answer questions and trusting the board not to get unnecessarily involved. They can also split up political allies when assigning individuals to particular projects or tasks (Sonnenfeld, 2002). Chairs can conduct a board evaluation in which members rate themselves, fellow directors, and the overall board. This works to identify any problematic actors and any factions that are forming.

CLASHING VIEWPOINTS ARE HEALTHY: HOW TO BANISH CONFORMITY

High-functioning boards are generally strongly united, but this does not mean unanimous agreement on every topic. Asking a challenging question or voicing a different opinion is not disloyal or dismissive. Minority viewpoints should be welcomed. A certain level of disagreement and tension is healthy and natural. Skeptics should be encouraged, as debate is a sign of a committed, strong board. Critical thinking is essential to anticipate problems, domino effects, and contingencies.

Building consensus is different from unquestioning groupthink. Consensus on a board involves discussion with members who hold different positions to reach common ground. This calls for surfacing issues, identifying themes and patterns, and devising and evaluating alternative solutions. Often, the groundwork happens outside formal meetings and may require a lot of behind-the-scenes communication and influencing.

Applying pressure is not the best approach. When constructive disagreement needs to reach a firm resolution, rather than questioning credentials or leaning on someone to be a team player, return to the principles of influence: Listen actively. Acknowledge all valid points. Present facts, examples, risks, and comparisons. Tie back to the common goal shared by the majority.

Finally, boards should allow members to save face as appropriate. Changing one's mind is a sign of openness and maturity. No one enjoys being humiliated or backing down, and phrasing statements in more neutral or generic terms can go a long way to taking the sting out of disagreements.

DISCOURAGING RIGIDITY AND STEREOTYPES

It is not uncommon for board members to fall into archetypes; peacemaker, contrarian, numbers person, big picture person, details person, etc. Stepping into other roles, especially on smaller boards, helps balance the workload and offers new perspectives.

The danger is becoming entrenched in a particular worldview, a limited way of seeing and thinking. Discussions that allow individuals to freely ask questions, share opinions, and consider options without the pressure of reaching a decision enhance engagement and understanding. These conversations reduce the impact of bias and promote better understanding without defensive rigidity.

Individually, board members should reflect on what they have in common with their fellow directors and cultivate empathy for them. Appreciate how divergent tastes and thoughts create a more engaging, dynamic board. Shy away from making assumptions or labeling others and lead with curiosity.

THE BEST KEPT SECRETS TO RUNNING A SUCCESSFUL NONPROFIT BOARD

We have already discussed the basic principles for operating a successful nonprofit board of directors. Now, let's delve into some lesser-known yet equally important aspects to keep in mind for ensuring the success of your board.

Clarify your board model and purpose: This applies at the initial stages but is worth returning to and revisiting periodically because it informs searches, nominations, elections, and ongoing operations. Will this be a board whose key focus is fundraising? A board providing guidance and oversight? A working board? A board that challenges and pushes management to new heights? A board that combines various styles?

Evolve over time: As a non-profit organization grows and changes in response to the community, the broader environment, or even public policy, its board may need to reshape itself to suit. Traditionally, boards seek directors with expertise in finance, marketing, human resources, legal, etc. But field-specific experience can also be valuable. Think of having teachers sit on an educational institute's board or social workers on a clinic's board. These experts offer vital insight to their fellow board members. In addition, experts in other complementary industries can assist the board in navigating competitive, demographic, or government shifts. No CEO can serve as the single source of information to a board. Although their view on the organization's critical issues is vital, diverse viewpoints are essential. A diverse board can work productively to steer the organization and set the agenda.

Use board members to open doors: Members can play a part in introducing their contacts–friends, colleagues, neighbors, family members–to the cause. Whether through low-touch methods like forwarding the organization's email updates or sharing appeals, there are many opportunities to connect new people with what your nonprofit does. This can extend to more involved tactics to showcase the work being done, like making introductions to the executive director, bringing guests to events, or giving people tours of the organization, to showcase. As a bonus, it allows others to develop an even stronger understanding and appreciation of active programs and projects.

Align committees strategically: Board committees are also often organized around functions. Innovative boards are moving toward structuring committees and working groups around strategic priorities. Taylor, Chait and Holland (1996) give the example of a seminary that oriented committees in line with its goals: globalizing the curriculum, improving relations with local churches, and providing continuing education. Another example was a women's college board that created councils as umbrellas for committee clusters to match business affairs, campus affairs, external affairs, and governance and board affairs.

Choose and track critical success metrics: As you know, finding ways to measure success is crucial. Showing visual and graphic representations of organizational progress, especially compared to past performance or external benchmarks, can be very impactful and galvanizing. Taylor, Chait & Holland (1996) suggest identifying 10 to 12 critical indicators of success: for starters, a hospital could monitor its rate of occupancy, while a museum might look at the return on endowment investments; an orchestra concerned about its aging supporter base might keep an eye on the size of its younger audience and whether ticket sales to this segment are trending up.

USEFUL TOOLS FOR NONPROFITS

As a nonprofit board member, your suggestions for tools and software can have a significant impact. Let's begin by exploring a list of productivity-enhancing tools worth considering for your organization.

Boardable is a digital platform for non-profit organizations and boards to manage and organize staff and volunteers, documents, meetings, and events. If managing these administrative aspects is becoming cumbersome or taking up too much time, Boardable is a tool that renders these tasks more efficient.

Donorbox is all-in-one fundraising software used by nonprofits around the world. Use it to add donation forms to websites or set up standalone donation pages; run varied campaigns, including events, peer-to-peer, crowdfunding, text, and membership campaigns; and store and maintain a donor database.

Double the Donation lets donors search for their employer and check if their donation is eligible for gift matching, and it is easy to integrate into your website. For the board, promoting its usage during fundraising events or campaigns can significantly enhance fundraising efforts by tapping into corporate matching programs.

Canva is invaluable for generating visual content to beef up your nonprofit's online presence. There are thousands of templates to design graphics for social media and other marketing channels. Create your brand kit and templates to ensure consistency with fonts, logos, and colors. Additionally, the board can encourage the marketing team to use Canva, promoting consistency and professionalism across all communication channels.

Trello can manage multiple projects and teams, maintaining a view of workflows and the status of various tasks. Assign items, set deadlines, upload files, add comments, and stay organized. It monitors progress on strategic initiatives, oversees committee tasks, and organizes meeting agendas. Furthermore, its integration capabilities with tools like Slack and Google Drive streamline board communication and file sharing, fostering efficient collaboration and transparency in board activities.

Slack is a versatile messaging platform that can enhance communication among nonprofit board members. It enables organized conversations through different channels related to various committees or projects. Channels can be private or open depending on confidentiality needs. Its call and screen-sharing capabilities enhance virtual meetings, while its integration with tools such as Trello and Google Drive improves workflow.

EveryAction was developed to meet the needs of nonprofits when it comes to managing relationships with prospects, supporters, and sponsors. Use it to set up and send emails with donation options, organize fundraisers online, engage followers and influencers, and track and report results. For board members, EveryAction can be particularly helpful as it provides a holistic view of fundraising activities and donor interactions, enabling them to monitor the effectiveness of these initiatives and make informed decisions about future strategies.

Another tool for communicating with your supporter base is **DonorView**. Features include managing and tracking contacts like donors and volunteers, sending communications and surveys to them, organizing peer-to-peer fundraisers or social campaigns, tracking donations, and more.

In this chapter, we've thoroughly examined the sensitive process of navigating a CEO transition. Though it's an event that doesn't happen frequently, it nevertheless requires thoughtful and careful management from the board to ensure the organization's stability and continuity. We emphasized the importance of balanced involvement from the board, encouraging an approach that avoids excessive meddling in daily operations yet still ensures strong oversight.

Furthermore, we delved into some common pitfalls that can challenge the effectiveness and unity of the board, including divisions within the group and the dangers of too much rigidity or excessive conformity. We emphasized the need for an open, collaborative environment that values diverse perspectives without compromising the board's unity and decision-making ability.

To wrap up, you've gained valuable tips and tools that will be highly beneficial for your board's operations. These resources can significantly improve your board's productivity and strategic effectiveness, and we recommend you keep them close as you continue to navigate the ever-evolving landscape of nonprofit governance. We hope these insights will guide you toward successful leadership and enable your nonprofit to thrive.

FINAL THOUGHTS

Nonprofit boards play a critical role in oversight and direction. They shape strategy and monitor its implementation, offer checks and balances to managerial decisions, oversee risk and compliance to avoid pitfalls, safeguard organizational culture, and ensure operations adhere to appropriate standards. As society and the nonprofit landscape evolve in these unpredictable and risk-laden times, board members' challenges will intensify, requiring greater commitment and effort from each individual.

Your mission-driven organization has likely been considering important matters such as environmental stewardship, social responsibility, organizational culture, diversity, and inclusion. As issues like environmental sustainability, regulatory changes, digital misinformation, and cybersecurity threats become more pressing, boards must stay updated and lead their organizations in effectively navigating these challenges.

Boards carry legal and ethical responsibilities for the organizations they govern. Their decisions and guidance depend mainly on the information provided to them, underscoring the importance of robust communication at the governance level. However, the ultimate accountability remains with the board. This book has laid the foundations for building a healthy nonprofit board to steer an organization through growing financial, technological, and social complexity.

The executive director, chair, and every board member have a crucial role in this system, and by understanding how to recruit, train, and support them, you will set every individual for success. Enhance the effectiveness of your board by seeking professionals known for their trustworthiness, strategic thinking, decisiveness, and analytical skills. These qualities significantly increase the likelihood of assembling a high-performing board. While no person can be expected to demonstrate mastery of every desirable skill, every director must be relied on to carry out their duties effectively.

Setting and communicating clear expectations around roles and responsibilities is the key to ensuring smooth operations, particularly regarding fundraising, audit, and other delicate matters. Address any signs of misconduct promptly and decisively, presenting a united stance. Remain vigilant for symptoms of stagnation in your board; if activities become routine or uninspired, initiate actions to bring in fresh ideas and enthusiasm, sparking renewed dedication and interest.

Refer back to Chapter Four anytime for a deeper examination of ten well-governed non-profit organizations and specific takeaways from each, many of which have been in the media spotlight for the right reasons. Remember, your board is on track when members uphold their central duties and respect the rules, bylaws, and conduct standards. It's also essential for the board to monitor and plan for both internal and external changes. With this proactive approach and dedication to ongoing adaptation, you can be assured that your board is effectively guiding your nonprofit toward its goals.

I hope you've found value in *Nonprofit Board Success: How to Build a Board of Directors So Good That Even the Top CEOs Would Be Jealous*. It means a lot to me to hear from my readers, and your feedback could inform others who are also striving to build successful boards for their nonprofits. If you could spare a moment to leave a review on Amazon or Audible, I'd really appreciate it. Your insights could make all the difference to someone else's journey. Thank you for your time and consideration. Wishing you and your board continued success!

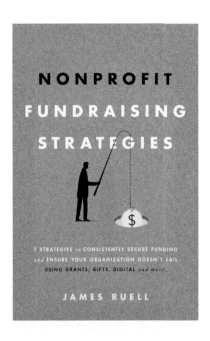

Nonprofit Fundraising Strategies: 7 Strategies to Consistently Secure Funding and Ensure Your Organization Doesn't Fail - Using Grants, Gifts, Digital and More...

The 12 Secrets of

Exceptional
Nonprofit
Leaders

The Key Traits Necessary to Drive Social Impact

James Ruell

The 12 Secrets of Exceptional Nonprofit Leaders: The Key Traits Necessary to Drive Social Impact

REFERENCES

Adediran, A. (2022). *Racial and ethnic diversity is lacking among nonprofit leaders – but there are ways to change that.* The Conversation. https://theconversation.com/racial-and-ethnic-diversity-is-lacking-among-nonprofit-leaders-but-there-are-ways-to-change-that-174490

Bambach, M. (2012). *Where has the Strategic Thinking Gone in the Nonprofit Board Room?* https://www.anzam.org/wp-content/uploads/pdf-manager/299_ANZAM-2012-221.PDF

BDO. (2018). *Governance.* https://www.bdo.com/insights/industries/governance

BoardAssist. (2015). *Board Recruiting Best Practices - Where and When should your board meet?* https://boardassist.org/blog/board-recruiting-best-practices-board-meet/

BoardAssist. (2019). *Top twelve tips for courting new board members.* https://boardassist.org/blog/top-twelve-tips-courting-new-board-members/

Boardable. (2023). *Board Fundraising: The role boards play in development.* https://boardable.com/resources/nonprofit-board-fundraising/

BoardPro. (2022). A complete guide to successful hybrid board meetings. *BoardPro.* https://www.boardpro.com/blog/a-complete-guide-to-successful-hybrid-board-meetings

BoardSource. (2012). Leading With Intent. https://leadingwithintent.org/wp-content/uploads/2021/06/2021-Leading-with-Intent-Report.pdf

Capacity Experts. (2021). *Lessons on pivoting.* https://www.capacityexperts.com/blog/7-Lessons-on-Pivoting-Based-on-Catholic-Charities-Diocese-of-Trenton-Nimble-Covid-19-Response

Center for Association Leadership. (2019). *The path to a more strategic board.* ASAE. https://www.asaecenter.org/resources/articles/

an_magazine/2019/january-february/the-path-to-a-more-strate
gic-board

Charity Navigator. (2023). *Accountability & Finance*. https://www.chari
tynavigator.org/about-us/our-methodology/ratings/accountabil
ity-finance/

Ciampa, D. (2016). *The Right Way to Bring a New CEO On Board.*
Harvard Business Review. https://hbr.org/2016/12/after-the-
handshake

Council of Nonprofits. (2023). *Board's role & audit committees.* https://
www.councilofnonprofits.org/running-nonprofit/nonprofit-audit-
guidec/boards-role-audit-committees

Deloitte. (2023). *Charity Audit Committee performance evaluation.* https://
www2.deloitte.com/uk/en/pages/charities-and-not-for-profit/arti
cles/charity-audit-committee-performance-evaluation.html

Freeman, K. W. (2019). *How to make sure your board sets a good example
for your company.* Harvard Business Review. https://hbr.org/2019/
02/how-to-make-sure-your-board-sets-a-good-example-for-your-
company

Grant Thornton. (2016). *Not-for-Profit Audit Committee Guidebook.*
https://www.grantthornton.com/content/dam/grantthornton/
website/assets/content-page-files/nfp/pdfs/2016/NFP-Audit-
committee-guide/nfp-audit-committee-guide.pdf

Guidestar. (2023). *Boy Scouts of America.* https://www.guidestar.org/
profile/43-0655866

Guidestar. (2023). *Boys & Girls Clubs of America.* https://www.
guidestar.org/profile/13-5562976

Guidestar. (2023). *Goodwill Industries International, Inc.* https://www.
guidestar.org/profile/53-0196517

GuideStar. (2023). *St. Jude Children's Research Hospital.* https://www.
guidestar.org/profile/62-0646012

GuideStar. (2023). *Step Up For Students.* https://www.guidestar.org/
profile/59-3649371

Guidestar. (2023). *The Nature Conservancy.* https://www.guidestar.org/
profile/53-0242652

Jansen, P., and Hatch, H. (2022). *Does your nonprofit board need a CGO?*

(*SSIR*). https://ssir.org/articles/entry/does_your_nonprofit_board_need_a_cgo

Johnson, E. (2006). *Compensation Committees: Does Your Organization Need a Compensation Committee?* https://www.whitefordlaw.com/siteFiles/news/compensation_committees_does_your_organization_need_a_compen_2.pdf

Kramer, P. (2018). *Top indicators of nonprofit Financial Health*. Nonprofit Finance Fund. https://nff.org/blog/top-indicators-nonprofit-financial-health

Martinelli, F. (2014). *Positioning your nonprofit board for Strategic Leadership - Part 2.* https://www.linkedin.com/pulse/20140604143745-24304469-positioning-your-nonprofit-board-for-strategic-leadership-part-2/

McAllister, S. (2021). *The Essential Keys to Being a Good Board Member.* https://www.elcinfo.com/cbi-blog/the-essential-keys-to-being-a-good-board-member

Meehan, W., and Jonker, K. (2019). How well does your nonprofit board measure up? *Forbes.* https://www.forbes.com/sites/meehanjonker/2019/04/02/how-well-does-your-nonprofit-board-measure-up

Mooney, R. (2021). Step Up Receives 4-star Rating From Charity Navigator For 15th Year. *Step up for Students.* https://www.stepupforstudents.org/blog/step-up-receives-4-star-rating-from-charity-navigator-for-15th-year/

Network for Good. (2023). *Board fundraising: 4 roles Your nonprofit's board must fill.* https://www.networkforgood.com/resource/board-fundraising/

Nonprofit Finance Fund. (2022). *State of the Nonprofit Sector Survey.* https://nff.org/learn/survey#results

Nonprofit Research Collaborative. (2012). *Engaging Board Members in Fundraising.* https://www.urban.org/sites/default/files/publication/25896/412673-The-Nonprofit-Research-Collaborative-Special-Report-Engaging-Board-Members-in-Fundraising.PDF

Prosper Strategies. (2023). *Boys & Girls Clubs of America.* https://pros

per-strategies.com/portfolio-posts/boys-and-girls-clubs-of-america/

Quigley, T., and Hambrick, D. (2012). *When the Former CEO Stays on as Board Chair: Effects on Successor Discretion, Strategic Change, and Performance.* https://www.jstor.org/stable/41524896

Shekshnia, S. (2018). *How to be a good board chair.* Harvard Business Review. https://hbr.org/2018/03/how-to-be-a-good-board-chair

Sintetos, T. (2022). Nonprofit Diversity, equity, and Inclusion: Key issues for today. *BoardEffect.* https://www.boardeffect.com/blog/nonprofit-diversity-equity-inclusion/

Snyder, H., Andersen, M., and Zuber, J. (2017). *Nonprofit Fraud: How Good Are Your Internal Controls?* https://www.sfmagazine.com/articles/2017/march/nonprofit-fraud-how-good-are-your-internal-controls/

Springly. (2022). *How Many Board Members Should My Nonprofit Have?* https://www.springly.org/en-us/blog/how-many-board-members-should-a-nonprofit-have/

St Jude. (2022). *Most trusted nonprofit.* https://www.stjude.org/media-resources/news-releases/2022-fundraising-news/most-trusted-nonprofit.html

Sonnenfeld, J. A. (2002). *What makes great boards great.* Harvard Business Review. https://hbr.org/2002/09/what-makes-great-boards-great

Sullivan, S. The Arizona Republic. (2021). Now available: Thousands of Smithsonian-produced learning guides available at nonprofits. *Arizona Republic.* https://www.azcentral.com/story/news/local/arizona-education/2021/06/13/smithsonian-institution-nonprofit-learning-guide-helps-students-amid-pandemic/7531216002/

Taylor, B. E. (1996). *The new work of the nonprofit board.* Harvard Business Review. https://hbr.org/1996/09/the-new-work-of-the-nonprofit-board

Travers, S. (2014). New Scrutiny of City's Library Trustees. *City Limits.* https://citylimits.org/2014/06/18/new-scrutiny-of-citys-library-trustees/

Tugman, L., and Leka, L. (2019). *5 Key factors to Enhance Audit Committee Effectiveness*. IFAC. https://www.ifac.org/knowledge-gateway/supporting-international-standards/discussion/5-key-factors-enhance-audit-committee-effectiveness

Tuomala, J., Yeh, D., and Smith, K. (2018). *Making Founder Successions Work (SSIR)*. https://ssir.org/articles/entry/making_founder_successions_work

Useem, M. (2oo6). *How Well-Run Boards make decisions*. Harvard Business Review. https://hbr.org/2006/11/how-well-run-boards-make-decisions

Vanguard. (2021). *Nonprofit Insights with St. Jude Children's Research Hospital*. https://www.vanguardcharitable.org/blog/nonprofit-insights-st-jude-childrens-research-hospital

Wire, A. (2022). *What is a compensation committee: Roles, responsibilities and best practices*. IR Magazine. https://www.irmagazine.com/esg/what-compensation-committee-roles-responsibilities-and-best-practices